MICHELLE ANTHONY

BECOMING A
SPIRITUALLY
HEALTHY
FAMILY

Avoiding the 6 Dysfunctional
Parenting Styles

David C Cook®

transforming lives together

BECOMING A SPIRITUALLY HEALTHY FAMILY
Published by David C Cook
4050 Lee Vance View
Colorado Springs, CO 80918 U.S.A.

David C Cook Distribution Canada
55 Woodslee Avenue, Paris, Ontario, Canada N3L 3E5

David C Cook U.K., Kingsway Communications
Eastbourne, East Sussex BN23 6NT, England

The graphic circle C logo is a registered trademark of David C Cook.

The website addresses recommended throughout this book are offered as a
resource to you. These websites are not intended in any way to be or imply an
endorsement on the part of David C Cook, nor do we vouch for their content.

Unless otherwise noted, all Scripture quotations are taken from the Holy Bible,
New International Version®, NIV®. Copyright © 1973, 2011 by Biblica, Inc. ™ Used
by permission of Zondervan. All rights reserved worldwide. www.zondervan.com;
ESV are taken from The Holy Bible, English Standard Version® (ESV®), copyright
© 2001 by Crossway, a publishing ministry of Good News Publishers. Used by
permission. All rights reserved; KJV are taken from the King James Version of
the Bible. (Public Domain); NKJV are taken from the New King James Version®.
Copyright © 1982 by Thomas Nelson, Inc. Used by permission. All rights reserved.
The author has added italics to Scripture quotations for emphasis.

LCCN 2014948795
ISBN 978-0-7814-1139-4
eISBN 978-0-7814-1141-7

The Team: Alex Field, Karen Lee-Thorp, Amy
Konyndyk, Helen Macdonald, Karen Athen
Cover Design: Nick Lee
Cover Image: iStockphoto

Printed in the United States of America
First Edition 2015

1 2 3 4 5 6 7 8 9 10

103014

BECOMING A SPIRITUALLY HEALTHY FAMILY

To Eileen Anthony, and
Ron and Verna Van Groningen
Your legacy continues!

Contents

1

The Director and the Script

Choosing the Abundant Life

When an actor plays a scene exactly the way a director orders, it isn't acting. It's following instructions.

James Dean

Imagine for a moment that you're a famous screenplay writer. And beyond that, the richest, most powerful executive producer. Well, let's not stop there … you can also direct! In fact, people from the entire globe are so enamored with you and your vast unprecedented skills that they await your very next movie. What will it be? With all your ability, power, and resources, what will you create?

What is the plot of this grand story you will tell? And, I wonder, will you include a part for yourself? Is it an obscure role just to see if people notice you, or will you place yourself smack in the middle of it as the main character? I mean, why not? It is in fact your story, isn't it? Shouldn't it be about you?

More and Better

We may not possess the skills or finances to chart such a course, but nevertheless, deep inside each one of us is the desire to write and control our own script of life. While most of us realize that much of life is truly out of our control, that does not stop us from trying—not one little bit. In fact, in the moments when we sense that someone else is sitting in the director's chair or framing a scene not to our liking or—heaven forbid—getting a better role than ours, we step in.

"CUT! That's not how I saw this scene playing out at all," you say, snorting. "You see, this character, *my* character, should have *more* ..."

"More?" asks the voice that comes from a shadowed Director's chair where you believe you ought to be sitting.

"Yes," you reply. "More. More lines, more opportunities, more beauty, wealth, success, and friends. And"—you continue with more passion in your voice than the first rebuttal—"better."

This time the Director remains silent.

That doesn't stop you. Instead, thinking that you have a convincing argument, you continue.

"A better marriage, better children, a better boss, job, house, car, and better family members."

Pleased that you have made your point, you pause for a response. Then the Director stands up and speaks.

"Do you want to be in *this* chair? Do you really want to be in charge? Do you think you can write, direct, and produce this story?"

Ignorant of the weight of the question, and drunk with the possibilities of writing this story of life the way you have always imagined, your answer is deliberate.

"Yes. As a matter of fact, I do."

Cease to Live

We've all had this moment, whether we recognize it or not. This attempt to take over the Director's chair.

We grab a pen, write a script, and try to steer the story in the direction we think it should go.

We have imagined our lives, ourselves, and our families as something different from what we have. We delude ourselves into thinking the script we have is deficient in some way—or that there must be some cosmic mix-up and we got handed the wrong one entirely. We compare our script to others, and we become dissatisfied with our part.

In that moment, we have forgotten the plot. We have forgotten the main Character. We have forgotten *why* this story was written and how we are a part of it in the first place. What we don't realize is that for all the creative abilities and gifts He's given us, the one thing God hasn't given us is the ability to envision the *whole story*.

But He can.

He's the only one who knows all the characters, understands the plotline, and is weaving them all together toward the ending He intends. He hasn't hired us to write our *own* stories; He has cast us in *His* story.

He invites us to surrender the pen and to live abundantly "on script" in the part He's written for us.

But often we choose to try to control the script ourselves … and when we do, *we cease to live.*

Now, I didn't say "die," because we continue to physically breathe, but we must understand that we do *stop living.* We stop living the life that He planned for us, and we start living out of dysfunction instead.

Jesus said that He came to give us life—and life *abundant.* Anything or anyone that keeps us from playing the part in the script that was handed to us keeps us from abundant life.

As you take a look at your life right now, and the lives of those in your family whom you love, you might be asking yourself, "What is the abundant life, anyway?" Well, the Bible seems to make a few things clear that may inform us on this topic:

- God is the Author and Director of the entire universe.
- God is in complete control and has authority of all things in heaven, on earth, and under the earth.
- God is the Giver and Sustainer of life. In Him all things exist, move, and breathe in order to bring glory to Him.
- God works all things together to accomplish His plans, and nothing or no one can ever thwart God's plan.
- And, oh, did I mention, God is perfection? He is perfect. His ways are perfect. And His plan is perfect.

Abundant Life or Dysfunctional Living?

Therefore, it seems that the abundant life is to seek and know this holy and perfect God, understand the plan He has initiated, discover how He is writing the story to accomplish this plan, and then humbly receive your script and play your part—*as written.*

Spiritually healthy families come from spiritually healthy individuals who, on their journey together, seek to live "on script" each day. Spiritually healthy families are not made up of people who never mess up their lines, or forget whether to enter stage left or stage right—they are not perfect performers. But they are families working together as loving cast members, discovering the intimate beauty of watching the character development of each person unfold—in the midst of the messiness.

The apostle Paul once wrote:

> Not that I have already obtained all this, or have already arrived at my goal, but I press on to take hold of that for which Christ Jesus took hold of me. Brothers and sisters, I do not consider myself yet to have taken hold of it. But one thing I do: Forgetting what is behind and straining toward what is ahead, I press on toward the goal to win the prize for which God has called me heavenward in Christ Jesus. (Phil. 3:12–14)

It's the pressing on toward the goal that is important, not simply trying to look perfect or be perfect. And it's also important to forget what is behind us, because we cannot change our pasts. We can, however, look forward and fix our eyes on Jesus as we listen to His direction.

We have to fix our eyes on Jesus because He is the only one who offers the abundant life—a by-product of following Him and participating in His kingdom. The abundant life is the beautiful fruit of pursuing Jesus, and it was never intended to be a pursuit in and of itself.

When we pursue Jesus, *we get the abundant life.*

When we pursue the abundant life, *we get dysfunction.*

Wow … that's not a difficult choice, is it? Yet it seems that our lives are so entangled in the pursuit of happiness, fulfillment, and abundance that ironically we often *don't get any of them.* Instead, we settle for (and simply manage) our dysfunction.

And isn't it strange how often we deal symptomatically with the dysfunctions in our lives rather than going directly to the source? In this book I have identified six dysfunctional parenting styles that I believe are the result of families pursuing "abundance" on their own and in their own strength. I will also unpack the remedies that God has offered us when we shift our pursuit to Him.

The Show Must Go On

As you read through the chapters in this book, you will see God's story—from the Bible and also from the lives of people in real families today. You will learn about individuals with whom you might identify. They flub their lines, they fall in the middle of important scenes, they sabotage others' parts in the story, they yell at the

Director and storm offstage, they get their scenes out of order, and they make useless calls to their agents who prove to be no help at all. And this is just one act of the play, mind you.

Many fail, and they fail miserably. And just when you're about to point at them and laugh or judge, I believe if you are honest, you will see yourself and your family in this story as well.

Each chapter not only identifies common parenting and family dysfunctions but also deals with each issue in a more generalized sense. While many of us find ourselves deeply burdened with issues of fear, control, and people-pleasing, *all* of us live in a world where these things are potential pitfalls on any given day.

But the most glorious thing that will astound you afresh is that the Director continues to shout, "The show must go on!" He doesn't throw up His hands in disgust. He doesn't walk away—ever. He simply, and lovingly, keeps writing this story in which His original plan miraculously remains intact despite our efforts to derail it.

Living on Script

In the midst of becoming a spiritually healthy family, there will be moments living on script when we'll see the genius of our Master Storyteller. We'll see Him weave in plot twists we never expected, redeem characters we had written off, and take the story places beyond all we could ask or imagine.

He continues to remind each actor along the way that this is a story of redemption and grace. This is also very much a story in which *we do have a choice*. We get to choose every day to pick up our script and either play it … or not.

Make no mistake: the story will continue. The story will succeed. But the real question is, will you be playing your part or not? So as you learn your role, listen to the Director. Release your grip on His chair. Focus on the script He has written for you.

Play the part He has assigned you to play. And fight for the abundant life He envisions for you and your family.

Reflect and Respond

1. Take assessment of your life and the lives of your family members right now. In what areas have you coveted another's script? In what ways have you attempted to play the role of Director in your own life?
2. Rate yourself today on a scale from 1 to 5 (1—"ceased to live" or "dysfunctional living" and 5—"living the abundant life"). What factors have contributed to this number?
3. What is most difficult for you in the process of "staying on script"?
4. What do you want or need to say to a God who continues to accomplish His plans despite our childish demands?
5. Where does your family need an intervention from God right now? Talk to your heavenly Father about this situation.

The Six Dysfunctions of Parenting

Omitting God from the Scene

A dysfunctional family is any family with
more than one person in it.
Mary Karr, *The Liar's Club*

Sin is a reality of our lives. Without God's love and forgiveness, the spiritually healthy family would be impossible. Without God's help, dysfunction is our only option.

Some dysfunction is the reality of living in an imperfect world with imperfect people, but it will be especially present when we omit God from our lives. Painful dysfunction comes when we choose to sit in the Director's chair in the attempt to live the abundant life in the way we see fit.

We must remember that the abundant life God has promised is the beautiful by-product that He alone offers when He writes and controls the script. He gives us significance and purpose in the midst of the imperfections of our family life when we follow our lines—*as written*.

However, let's for a moment take God out of the picture. Frightening, perhaps, but something we actually do without even thinking about it. When we choose to "go it alone" in this thing called parenting, the result is inevitable dysfunction that has no promise of the abundant life. While there are probably hundreds, if not thousands, of types of dysfunction in today's families, let's unpack six dysfunctional parenting styles that without God's redemption will leave a negative impact on our families. In the following chapters we will see God's remedy for each of them.

The Six Dysfunctional Parenting Styles

- The Double-Minded Parent
- The I-Can't-Say-No Parent
- The Driver Parent
- The Micro-Managing Parent
- The Criticizing Parent
- The Absentee Parent

The Double-Minded Parent

Some may call you a Double-Minded parent, but you call it being *emotionally healthy*. After all, just because you are a Christian, what is wrong with making sure that you are whole and happy and indulge in all that this life has to offer? You see adulthood as a time to fulfill all your dreams in this life, and your children are just one small part of those dreams. You think about how wonderful it is to have all that God offers, as well as what the world offers too! These are the mantras that you live by:

- "I have worked hard my whole life—now it's time for me!"
- "God wants me to be happy, so I know that He is okay with my making choices that fulfill my needs even over my children's, because their day will come when they are older."
- "Who says you can't have it all?"
- "Of course I love God, but this world is pretty cool too, don't you think?"

As a Double-Minded *mom*, you have a limited perspective of life. You truly believe that the story line is about you, because, after all, you are in every scene!

After making it through the first few decades of life (which were exhausting), you now have the means and the "moxie" to let your star shine the brightest. You must have the latest and the greatest, and no one is going to stop you. Children are sometimes an asset because they make adorable models in Christmas cards and allow you to brag in the social scene, but they can also equally cramp your style when you desire to stay out late or get away somewhere exotic for the weekend.

As a Double-Minded *dad*, you are equally susceptible. You struggled climbing the corporate ladder and now finally have a chance to make a name for yourself. After "paying your dues," it's now time to have the title, the perks, and the admiration from onlookers. You have to have the biggest house, the most expensive toy, or the latest technology. Sure, you travel a lot, but you have earned it. You deserve some peace and quiet, and want time away to enjoy the best golf courses and the finest dining.

Children raised by the Double-Minded parent will often grow up having codependent tendencies, seeking acceptance from others, being unrealistic in their view of "self," and feeling insecure. They are confused about what it means to follow Christ, and might avoid their parents in adulthood.

The I-Can't-Say-No Parent

The world is such a negative place. The home should be a positive place where one can say "Why not?" I-Can't-Say-No parents love to say yes because when they do, everyone seems happy. These parents think that becoming a mom or dad is a perfect way to expand their social life as well. They truly enjoy the company of their children and don't see a need for hierarchy in the family sector.

In order to cultivate a "friendship" from an early age with their children, these parents make sure that they confide in their children and seek their opinions at every turn. These parents also sacrifice many personal opportunities for the sake of their children's needs. An I-Can't-Say-No parent might try to justify his or her actions by saying:

- "I want to give my child all that I didn't have when I was growing up."
- "Discipline is exhausting for me and my child—so I don't do it! I create no boundaries, and therefore there is no need. Besides, I really, really, really want my kids to like me."
- "Unpopular no more, I now have a junior companion in life!"
- "Sure, I rely on my child for emotional and social support—that's what friends do!"
- "In order to create intimacy and trust, I don't have any boundaries on the topics that I discuss with my child."
- "I had a kid because I want to spoil someone. I like to spend money and be generous—what's so bad about that?"
- "My child is very mature for her age."

As the I-Can't-Say-No parent, you hate conflict. If you say no, there is almost always someone who gets upset, so it's better to just keep the peace. Besides, when your kids are more mature than most, you don't have to create as many boundaries. Sure, you wish they were more respectful and did more around the house, but their lives are very stressful, and anything you can do to ease their pain is worth it.

This positive parenting approach is often criticized by others. These critics say you don't have a backbone and your children are taking advantage of you. Your amiable style of parenting is often the result of your own codependent tendencies and ensures that your dysfunction will fill in the gaps of any and all other forms of dysfunction too! Win-win!

Or perhaps friendship with peers was difficult for you when you were growing up. Therefore, you now have the chance to cultivate friendships with your children, who will not be "fair-weather" or leave you for another set of friends. This dysfunction is rooted in feelings of inadequacy and an inability to relate with people your own age. Your children and your children's friends think you're cool, smart, and fun. "Perhaps I am just young for my age, and my peers don't get me," you rationalize.

When your kids get older and choose their peers over you, you find yourself desperate to keep their affection. You resort to buying their time and attention or guilting them into it. Either way you must ensure that you will not be without their companionship because you are afraid of being alone or unloved.

Children raised by the I-Can't-Say-No parent often grow up too quickly, suffer from chronic boredom, think that rules don't apply to them, become poor money managers, are unable to cultivate healthy emotional boundaries with others, and have an unhealthy attachment to you in adulthood.

The Driver Parent

While the parent who has always been referred to as "driven" will see this as a compliment, others will label this way of parenting with a raised eyebrow of judgment. If you are a Driver parent, you view being driven as the secret to your success, and you want this same success (if not more) for your child. You wonder why people are always telling you to "lighten up" in the way you interact with your child, while you conjure up these justifications:

- "I am driven and have been successful, so why would I let my child waste one second of his day?"
- "Childhood is overrated—we need to start thinking of college now!"
- "I love to vicariously live through my child's life. It makes me so much more of an involved parent when I feel that we are "both" succeeding!"
- "Everyone else is my daughter's competition— and they had better get out of the way. There's room for only one at the top."

As the Driver, you are just that—you are the one making sure that this "vehicle" of a child is going somewhere. And that when he arrives, he is first. There are no winners in second place.

Driver parents often come from two extremes: as children, they themselves were high achievers, and are determined to keep the *legacy* alive; or they were not afforded the opportunities to succeed and now want to ensure that their children have those things. In either scenario, children of Driver parents often feel undue pressure to not disappoint their parents' expectations.

Parents can reveal their driven-ness in any arena of life, but Driver parents most commonly reveal themselves in sports and academics. In sports, success is often subjective, so the Driver parent is present at all the games or events to make sure that the coach and the child have the parent's perspective in the matter. In academics, success is objective; therefore great attention is given to study time, test scores, and advanced-placement courses (which will look good on college applications).

Children raised by the Driver parent will often grow up feeling anxious or depressed (or both), and dissatisfied with their accomplishments. They often struggle with addiction and are unable to "play" or relax.

The Micro-Managing Parent

As the Micro-Managing parent, you desire only the best for your kids. Because you are the adult and they are the children, how could your kids possibly know what is best for them? You have made some good (and bad) decisions in your life, and why wouldn't you want to pass on this wisdom to your children? After all, your "dysfunction" (as some would call it) comes from a well-meaning place in your heart. These are statements you might use to reassure yourself you are on the right track:

- "I know what is right. It's my job to make sure my child doesn't make a mistake!"
- "Everything is done the way I want it, or I do it myself. Since my standards are so high, it's just easier that way for everyone."
- "My kids don't understand that I make all their decisions for their own good."

- "The world is a dangerous place—period!
Someday my kids will thank me for protecting
them."

As the Micro-Manager, you need to be in control of *everything*. Your parenting style reflects your fear of letting go and what could happen if you do. The exaggerated need to be in charge of everyone and every decision is a dysfunction that stems from insecurity. Perhaps you were wounded as a child, and now, by your control, you ensure that you will never be victimized again. You now have a voice and will control circumstances by force, manipulation, and guilt in order to arrange life's events in such a way that you come out on top as the "victor."

This type of insecurity can be hard to detect because it often looks brash and arrogant on the outside. But underneath the surface, deep down, those who *must* be in control are those who are really wounded and are fearful of being wounded again.

Children raised by the Micro-Managing parent will often grow up doubting themselves, feeling driven to perfection, struggling with headaches and stomachaches, and developing eating disorders.

The Criticizing Parent

The Criticizing parent is one who can't help but point out what is wrong. To him or her, it's obvious what needs to be fixed, and consequently this parent calls attention to the problem so it can be corrected. As a Criticizing parent, you argue that this is a gift to your child, while others say you are being cruel with your words. You question how else your child will get the "thick skin" needed to survive in a harsh world and believe that you're doing her a favor by "toughening" her up.

To feel reassured, a Criticizing parent might make these justifications:

- "Life is tough. I didn't get a free pass; why should he?"
- "Of course I constantly criticize my child (even in public). It keeps her ego under control."
- "I never praise my child because then he will strive for better. It's the only way to get ahead in this life."
- "I don't encourage my child's interests—she will probably change her mind soon anyhow. What a waste of time and money."
- "If I don't point out his faults, someone else will. Wouldn't he rather it come from me than from a stranger?"

Criticism is just a way for you to keep the "family business" going. You were most likely criticized as a child, as were your parent(s) and your grandparent(s). This heritage has built in you a certain heartiness that doesn't have time to feel emotions, whine about the past, or spend time crying over what is not. This hard outer shell is used to help hide the heartbreaking disappointments and shame-filled memories of your past. Rather than expose the hurt and deal with it, you find it easier and more effective to keep it locked away safely where no one can mess it up any further.

Children raised by the Criticizing parent will often grow up bullying others, feeling insecure, blaming others for their mistakes, and being pessimistic about the future.

The Absentee Parent

The Absentee parent is just that—absent from the daily events of their children's lives. In your mind the big moments in life are not losing teeth, hitting a home run in Little League, or a dance recital. The big moments are the ones that you are providing and planning for, such as college, weddings, and retirement. You can justify your absence because of the following reasons:

- "I recognize that my child would rather have all today's 'stuff' than me, so I work long hours to provide for his current and future needs."
- "My absence is a good way for my children to learn independence."
- "My nanny (or babysitter) is younger and more fun than I am."
- "I deny my child emotional bonding when I am home so that our time away is easier on her."

Being an Absentee parent is actually a sacrifice that you feel is justified by your love for your family. Even though they complain about you *not being around* more, you believe that if you were there, they would complain about *not having* more. In your mind it's a lose-lose situation, so you have picked the lesser evil. You tell yourself that your children are fine because you know they are in the hands of a wonderful primary caregiver and they always look happy in the pictures you view online.

Absenteeism is birthed from an insatiable need to achieve and succeed. A parent with this dysfunction has no boundaries on time and energy, and feels that sleep and rest are for weak people. Absentee parents pride themselves on working long hours and measure success by how many hours over forty they put into a workweek. While they boast of an eighty-hour workweek, feeling proud of their accomplishments, they simply can't understand those who find satisfaction in a job well done *and* also find time for recreation, rest, and service to others. They justify their dysfunction by criticizing others' lack of ambition, work ethic, or inability to progress.

Children raised by an Absentee parent often grow up too fast, become sexually promiscuous, have low self-worth, and demand inordinate attention from others.

There's Hope!

In contrast to the six dysfunctional parenting styles stands the offer of hope from God that we may live in relationship with Him, pursuing His kingdom while living on His script. While far from perfect, the Spiritually Healthy parent is a parent who walks each day, step by step, with God as his or her guide.

Becoming a spiritually healthy family means you will allow God to call the shots for you and your family members and that you look to Him to give you wisdom instead of relying on your own strength and "great ideas". Because you realize you are a work in progress yourself, you offer your children grace when needed, while helping them see the correct path that God desires all His children to follow.

You recite the following things each day, because, deep down you know them to be true:

- "I recognize that my child has been entrusted to me by God and that I need His guidance to raise her."
- "I know I live in a sinful world, but I will seek to put God's character on display in my home in everyday situations."
- "I know there is a higher calling as a parent than controlling my child's behavior—and that is forming his faith."
- "I seek to grow spiritually myself, knowing that the overflow of this will have a positive impact on my child."

Children raised by the Spiritually Healthy parent often grow up knowing God, loving others, living a life of meaning, and recognizing that this world is not their ultimate home.

What to Expect

The following six chapters will take each of the dysfunctional parenting styles and unpack its reality in light of today's family as well as investigate its potential redemption when offered to God in submission to His script.

Let me be clear that becoming spiritually healthy in an area of dysfunction brought to light in the upcoming chapters will not be a matter of reading a chapter and then saying, "Oh, now I get it—I'm good to go." The six chapters are designed to help you put a finger on issues that need attention in your ongoing spiritual health. The kind of formation discussed in this book will be a *process* in which the Holy Spirit will work on you (and with you) "deep down" over time.

If you recognize yourself in a given chapter, the themes should become fodder for ongoing prayer, discussion with trusted friends, and Bible investigation and meditation. Don't become discouraged when the change you desire is not immediate; stopping a dysfunctional pattern is a process that takes time.

I want you to have hope. Not only are hope and faith needed for the change process to begin, but they also help fuel the continued work and transformation that takes place over the long haul. In the change process, we first need a "moment of honest truth" when we recognize and admit our dysfunction or shortfall. Then we must grieve what has been lost in the midst of that dysfunction. After a season of grief, we begin to desire a better way. With dependence on God through His Spirit, I pray you will envision that better way—His way.

The future you envision will be your compass to keep you on course. When you veer off track or fail, remember that change is not an all-or-nothing process. When you have a day that is less than successful, it's just that—*a day*. Tomorrow offers the hope of making the changes you envisioned together with your heavenly Father. Remember that God's mercies are new every morning. During the change process, this is incredibly good news!

I believe that as you *make choices* to allow transformation to occur in your life and in your family, and as you become a renewed person through God's help and love, there will come a day when you will look back at your former self and barely recognize him or her. The change that Jesus Christ offers is truly miraculous. Knowing this is possible for you and your family members is part of the faith you need as you embark on this journey.

Lastly, the final two chapters of this book will unveil a glimpse of what it means to walk in grace as you become a Spiritually Healthy parent (and family) and live the abundant life God has for you. You also will have opportunities to create milestones to mark this incredible, live-giving journey along the way so that your story will be told in the lives of your children for generations to come!

So let's get started. Let's take the plunge into discerning the realities of our lives and our families as they are today, knowing that whatever we discover is of no shock to our heavenly Father. He knows it *all* and loves us *no matter what*.

Reflect and Respond

Before reading the next chapters, pause to assess your own family of origin. Review the six dysfunctions discussed in this chapter, and then take a moment to answer the following questions:

1. Which dysfunction best describes how you were parented?
2. How has that dysfunction shaped the person and parent you are today?

3. What potential flaws in your character or in the way you interact with others need healing from this dysfunction?

4. In what ways has God redeemed that dysfunction? In what ways can He use its manifestations in your life for good?

5. What dysfunctions do you see yourself repeating in your role as a parent? In what ways are you compensating for your parents' dysfunction by swinging the pendulum the other way?

6. How will you submit these things to God, your Father, today?

3

Kissing the World Good-Bye

For the Double-Minded Parent

---

*One might as well try to ride two horses moving in
different directions, as to try to maintain in equal force
two opposing or contradictory sets of desires.*
Robert Collier

We live in a highly pressured, value-polarized world. The pace, the
tension, and the problems modern families face on a daily basis are
creating very real health issues for parents and children alike. At
every age our minds and hearts are being seduced to follow this, pay
attention to that, emulate so-and-so, and accumulate such-and-such.
It's no wonder that we drop in bed exhausted, but even then we have
trouble sleeping.

Simply speaking, our hearts are divided. We want to follow God and His best for us, but the reality of living *in* this world but living *for* God and His kingdom is difficult. The result is that our lives are filled with anxiety. We commonly feel guilty that we aren't doing enough or that we have indulged too much. Does this kind of tension sound even remotely familiar? If it does, you are not alone. Not only that, our heavenly Father told us this would be our condition. Time and time again, God tells us the allegiance of our hearts will be a battlefield.

The "Jesus Plus" Version

As we read Scripture, we see a common thread in the message that Jesus taught: "Follow me and no other." Our ears hear Him say, "Seek first the kingdom of God and His righteousness, and all these things shall be added to you" (Matt. 6:33 NKJV).

When we hear this, we may immediately fixate on the word "all." But Jesus doesn't define "all" in the way *we would* define "all." Jesus wants our whole hearts—all our attention, affection, allegiance—and in giving such, we receive *all* of Him and His kingdom. Yet a modern look at the Christian family has us chasing after *all* this world offers—*and* we want a little bit of Jesus too, because that's good, right?

We see it in our children, and we see it in ourselves. We want the "Jesus Plus" version. The version that will allow us to have our Jesus cake and eat it too. Yet the problem with this is that God has always said we must *choose.*

- Joshua 24:15: "But if serving the LORD seems
  undesirable to you, then choose for yourselves

this day whom you will serve, whether the gods your ancestors served beyond the Euphrates, or the gods of the Amorites, in whose land you are living. But as for me and my household, we will serve the LORD."

- Mark 8:34: "Then he called the crowd to him along with his disciples and said: 'Whoever wants to be my disciple must deny themselves and take up their cross and follow me.'"
- Exodus 20:3: "You shall have no other gods before me."

Jesus also said something in Matthew 6:24 that makes it abundantly clear that we must choose:

No one can serve two masters. Either you will hate the one and love the other, or you will be devoted to the one and despise the other. You cannot serve both God and money.

People-Pleasing Pressure

You may not consider yourself a "double-minded" person, but have you ever tried pleasing differing viewpoints? When we try to please differing value systems, we, in essence, are indulging ourselves by trying to play in two competing arenas. *We cannot win.* I remember when my children were little, I tried to please everyone who was watching me. I was a young parent and desperately wanted to "get it right."

One of the more confusing aspects of child rearing for me was discipline. I scoured books for wisdom and found that some well-intentioned authors shared a "spare the rod and spoil the child" approach, while others were in complete opposition to spanking, saying, "hands are for loving, not for hurting."

I personally knew Christian leaders and pastors on both ends of the spectrum. Then there were parents, in-laws, and friends. Each had their own method of how they thought my husband and I *should* discipline our kids.

Trying to please them all was overwhelming. I guess I thought that taking a middle-of-the-road approach would appease the majority of them, so I decided to use a wooden spoon if I needed to discipline my son. He was three at the time and possessed a gentle spirit. Rarely did I actually need to use the wooden spoon, for the mere sight of it was enough to get the corrected action I was asking for.

One night, while friends from our church were over for dinner, my son, Brendon, continued to disobey me by not staying in his bed. He got up to go the bathroom, to say "I love you" (my personal manipulative favorite), and for a hug, a scary sound, or a drink of water—you know the drill. It had gone too far, and I knew it. The glaring glances across the table told me that our guests thought I was not doing such a great job at this parenting gig. So I got up, indignant, to find my wooden spoon.

The wooden spoon was nowhere to be found. Knowing that all I usually needed to do to enforce obedience was to simply show my son that I was holding the wooden spoon, I went to the kitchen to find an alternative. The spoon had come in a companion set of other wooden utensils. So I picked up the wooden meat tenderizer. "He's *three*," I told myself. I'll simply hold the mallet in my hand and show him the wooden dowel. He'll think it's the spoon.

Well, I went in his room, as planned, holding up the wooden dowel, firmly telling him to get in his bed. And he did—*lickety-split*. We didn't hear from him again the entire night. I guessed it worked. Until the next morning at church.

I was serving as the children's ministry director at my church at the time, and I dropped off Brendon in his little preschool room for the morning. After the service I was making the rounds to check on all my classrooms and volunteer leaders. The leader from my son's room asked if she could talk to me *privately*. That's not usually a good thing.

She said, "Michelle, I'm a little concerned. Today, during prayer request time, Brendon asked that his mommy wouldn't hit him with a *hammer*!" A hammer? Oh my. I gasped out loud, but then the only thing I could think to say was, "Oh, but it wasn't a *hammer*; it was a *meat tenderizer*." Did I really say that? As if that were somehow better!

If we have parented for any amount of time, we know the feeling of being watched, judged, and questioned. Let's face it, parenting is tough, but it's even tougher when we are trying to please multiple voices in our heads. And at the root of a Double-Minded parent is the need to have it all—to have and please the world and God at the same time.

Our spiritual lives are similar. We find ourselves (and our children do too) entertaining and trying to appease multiple voices of success, beauty, and popularity. We are constantly in a tug-of-war of competing values and desires. But, in the quest for following Jesus, it is intensified, because we are not dealing with just *differing* perspectives—we are dealing with *opposing* worldviews. We can easily become the "Stretch Armstrong" in the middle.

Is there any hope, or do we just have to settle for the angst of being pulled in different directions?

God's Plan: Do Not Worry

Jesus offers a remedy for the self-absorbed individual, beginning in Matthew 6:25. He said, "Therefore"—because you cannot please both God and this world's system—"*do not worry.*"

Really? The remedy for living in a high-stressed world focused on self is to *not worry*?

It sounds too simplistic. But in actuality, the root of the word translated as "worry" here means to be fractured, pulled in two directions, or even cut into pieces. I think most of us can relate to these words. *It's the duplicity of our hearts and minds that breeds anxiety.* It occurs when we aren't focused.

There is a double-mindedness in us because our hearts truly desire *both*. We desire both God *and* this world. We love to indulge our lives with things, food, privileges, money, respect, popularity, addictive substances, and sex.

We know from James 1:8 that a person asking for wisdom but not having faith "is double-minded and unstable in all they do." I definitely feel unstable at times—as if I'm barely holding on for dear life. But, there is a lot vying for my attention and plenty to worry about. So much so that I can justify my anxiety.

The Entitlement of Worry

Before we dive into what we are worrying about as parents and grandparents, let's think about Jesus's statement. It's a command against something that many of us feel is involuntary. I mean, I don't normally think I *choose* anxiety. I've never said to my husband, "Honey, I'm going to take some time to go for a walk and just focus on how I can make myself feel utterly out of control and stressed out. I will fixate on all the things I'm unhappy about or I can't change in my life, and hopefully when I return, I will be a raving lunatic."

That would be ridiculous. But, if you think about it, Jesus states this as if it is indeed a *choice*.

Do not worry.

It's a command from Jesus to live in His kingdom as His followers.

There are things in this life that can cause us to worry: that surprise bill we don't have the means to pay or that call we never want to receive from the doctor's office. Yet Jesus seems to have the audacity to say, "But don't."

Surely He will understand worrying about some of these circumstances, right? I sometimes feel *entitled* to worry, don't you?

When we choose to follow Jesus, we have to live this life we have chosen on *His terms* and *His conditions*. We either choose to indulge ourselves and our desires, which brings the companion of anxiety, or we choose Jesus. One thing I have found to be true is that it's not very easy to live for a kingdom without knowing the king. When we choose the King, we must know Him in order to choose the way He wants us to live.

Choosing the King

Let's recap: "Therefore, do not worry." We realize that the life God wants for us and for our family members is a life that is focused on Him and not our "stuff." Worry is the condition of trying to please too many voices or masters and going after all that "stuff." Being focused on Jesus means we need to know Him and know His voice. Because Jesus is calling us to choose, this act of focus is the first step in making this choice.

Let me illustrate this. My son is grown now and recently worked at a camp as a recreation leader. One of his jobs was to lead people through a high-ropes course in the forest. My friends and I decided that we would do this and conquer our fears together. At one point in the course, I became filled with anxiety.

My legs were shaking. My heart was pounding. And I didn't think I could traverse the large space between two trees by walking on a tightrope with just my harness loosely holding me. My friends were trying to offer encouragement and advice, each of them shouting a different solution. Paralyzed by fear, all I could do was look down and focus on how far away I was from the ground.

Just then, my son leaped through the trees with monkey-like agility and arrived about six paces in front of me on the rope. "Mom," he said, "look at me. Keep your eyes on me and walk toward me." As he talked me through each step, I just fixed my gaze on him and where I was headed with him, instead of the world below. Eventually, I made it to the other side, victorious.

That moment reminds me of our spiritual journey with Jesus. We find ourselves completely paralyzed by our surroundings and all the competing messages shouting in our heads, and the more we fixate on them and the "world below," the more we are filled with anxiety. Instead, the author of the book of Hebrews told us to fix "our eyes on Jesus." We will need to train ourselves to do this in order to run the race that this life in Christ has set before us.

The Choice of Good or Better

It's the "fixing" part that is hard for us. We naturally think of ourselves first. We become self-absorbed, and *fixation* is to do anything and everything to please what is shouting inside us for attention.

In addition, our family members are multitasking, and we live in a world that assumes we can and will do multiple things at the same time. It's perfectly acceptable to *not focus*. Yet the spiritually healthy family will need to learn to stay focused not only on Jesus but also on the kind of life He has called us to. This is a life in contrast to the Double-Minded parent's inclination, because it's a life of self-denial. Jesus said in Mark 8:34, "Whoever wants to be my disciple must deny themselves and take up their cross and follow me."

There are three parts to this verse that are difficult for a Double-Minded parent. The first is to *deny self*. To say no to our flesh and its desires takes discipline and the power of God's Spirit. The second is to *take up our crosses*. The cross is symbolic for death. Death to self. Death to entitlement. In order to die to self, we must live for Christ. This is the third part—to follow Jesus. What we die for must be replaced by something more worthwhile and fulfilling in order to be sustainable.

Those three things remind us that becoming a spiritually healthy family means we will have to choose between right and wrong in order to live holy lives that are set apart from the world. And it also means we will need to choose between the "good" and the "better."

You see, whether we choose righteous living on any given day or not, most of us have a sense of what is right and wrong. But the choice between *good* and *better* is often more difficult. It is good to have our kids in sports and music and friend groups. It is good for us to serve at our kids' schools, participate in Bible studies, and have guys' nights out. It's good to serve in our communities, learn new skills, and work out. The lists go on and on. There is a lot of good out there. But at some point, when do we choose the *better*? And how do we determine what is the better when we simply want more "stuff"?

Wisdom from Above

Only wisdom from God about my specific life and the lives of the children He has entrusted to me will allow me to answer this question. If I look to my friends or family members to make these decisions, I will most likely be misguided. Because, in the struggle to determine what is good and what is better, only God can inform me from a perfect and loving perspective. What is good or better for someone else or someone else's children is not necessarily what is good or better for me. Wisdom comes from being in relationship with God and discerning His voice above all the other voices clamoring for my attention.

In the same way that our family relationships are built and strengthened by spending quality time (as well as quantity of time) together, our relationships with God are strengthened as we spend time in His Word, prayer, and other spiritual disciplines together.

Remember also that God's Word confidently tells us,

> If any of you lacks wisdom, you should ask God, who gives generously to all without finding fault, and it will be given to you. But when you ask, you must believe and not doubt, because the one who doubts is like a wave of the sea, blown and tossed by the wind. That person should not expect to receive anything from the Lord. Such a person is double-minded and unstable in all they do. (James 1:5–8)

Did you catch that? God wants us to ask for wisdom with expectation and faith. Otherwise He warns us that our doubting and our double-mindedness will make us unstable in all we do. This sounds a lot like how we feel in the midst of the dysfunction of chasing God and the world too. We feel unstable and unsatisfied. We desperately need God's wisdom in order to bring health and stability to our lives.

The Heart of Our Faith

Just when we are about to digest this idea of being focused on Jesus and not torn by the seductive words of this world, He adds another phrase to this verse, "Therefore …, do not worry *about your life*" (Matt. 6:25).

Well, that about sums it up. That's everything last time I checked. There's no wiggle room for the kids, my marriage, my job, my health, my reputation. It's my entire life. Of course, He goes on to list specifics just in case I didn't get the message the first time:

- what you eat and drink (basic sustenance of life)
- your body (my health, my appearance, my desires/needs, thoughts, emotions, feelings)
- what you will wear (while fashion is a natural twenty-first-century Western reading of this statement, sustainability is at stake for most in this world)

These essentials of life get to the *heart of our faith*.

Wilderness-Anything

Let's look at a biblical example of faith formation from the Old Testament. After the Hebrew people were freed from Egyptian slavery by God's miraculous power, they found themselves in the wilderness, en route to the Promised Land God was giving them as a gift so that they could freely worship Him alone.

"Wilderness-anything" refines our faith and commitment to God. It's those moments when the sun isn't shining on our faces, our confidence has eroded, and our futures look uncertain. In these moments our faith is put to the test. It's also the time that we see clearly how we have placed indulgent value in striving after the things of this world instead of aligning our hearts toward God.

The Hebrew people are referred to as Israelites as they begin their forty-year journey. What is interesting to remember is that this journey, from Egypt to the Promised Land, should have taken just a little over a week. Yet, because of their grumbling and complaining, along with their lack of faith, God determined that there was some work to be done in them spiritually.

These were a people who had forgotten who they were in many respects. After living for more than four hundred years in Egypt as slaves and being seduced by thousands of Egyptian gods, they had forgotten what it meant to have a relationship with Yahweh, *the one true God.*

By showing His power, God began to remind them that He is omnipotent over all false gods. He provided water from a rock, daily manna (a perfect food source) from the sky, and direction from a pillar of cloud or a pillar of fire. And of course, He began this journey with the parting of the Red Sea.

The result of this "time out" in the wilderness was a new generation, led by Joshua, who knew and trusted God. They entered the Promised Land and began to fight battles against God's enemies, finding themselves victorious as they kept their eyes and hearts focused on God. When they became enamored with their own abilities or ideas, they inevitably failed.

Sound familiar? We and our children seem to have seasons of "getting it" or being awakened to this life God has for us, but then we lose our focus and become distracted by our successes or seduced by the successes of others, and when we do that, we most assuredly will fail.

My Biggest Enemy

We have a very real Enemy who seeks "to steal and kill and destroy" us (John 10:10). Our Enemy, Satan, will distort and distract us away from the abundant life Jesus offers. As a Double-Minded parent, you must be aware that you cannot please both God and this world (or the Enemy in it). You will need to be able to discern between the two voices.

- **God says**, "Be holy and set apart for My glory and your good." **The Enemy says**, "Pornography, lust, and sex are for your satisfaction, and you deserve it. Who are you really hurting anyway?"
- **God says**, "Marriage is a covenant and declares the unity between Christ and My church." **The Enemy says**, "If you aren't happy or fulfilled, you deserve to get out. It's old-fashioned to think of marriage as a sacred vow."
- **God says**, "Each member of your family is made in My image, and I have made you My very own. I love you no matter what." **The Enemy says**, "You are not good enough now, and you will never be good enough for God … Who are you trying to fool?"
- **God says**, "Come and be with Me, talk to Me, listen to Me, worship Me. I will renew you and give you strength." **The Enemy says**, "Who has time for that? You need to get *everything* done … *and more*, because you are still not doing enough!"
- **God says**, "I love you and have created a part for you to play in My Story." **The Enemy says**,

"That's a crummy part! Have you seen so-and-
so's part? It's a much better role, and that's why
she is so happy. Write your own script!"

- **God says**, "Because of Jesus and what He did
  on the cross, I no longer hold your sin against
  you." **The Enemy says**, "What a loser you are.
  You keep making the same choices and commit-
  ting the same sins. You must not be a Christian
  anyway."

In his book *The Screwtape Letters*, C. S. Lewis described how a senior
demon is mentoring his young nephew on how to bring opposition to
Christians who endeavor to follow God (the demons' "Enemy") and His
ways. The older demon instructs his nephew with these words:

> Never forget that when we are dealing with any
> pleasure in its healthy and normal and satisfying
> form, we are, in a sense, on the Enemy's ground. I
> know we have won many a soul through pleasure.
> All the same, it is His invention, not ours. He made
> the pleasures: all our research so far has not enabled
> us to produce one. All we can do is to encourage the
> humans to take the pleasures which our Enemy has
> produced, at times, or in ways, or in degrees, which
> He has forbidden.[1]

God has offered us an abundant life as we pursue Him and His
kingdom. This "abundance" is distorted by our Enemy as he tells us

to take those gifts and use them in our lives in distorted ways that distract us from our focus on Jesus. Today, as an act of single focus of mind and heart to God, we can declare that only what God says is truth and that the lies of the Enemy have no place in our homes or lives.

Reflect and Respond

1. Think of a few words to describe your life and the lives of your family members right now. Are these words filled with anxiety and stress or peace and contentment?

2. In what ways have you become distracted with pleasing the people and the systems of this world, and in doing so have lost your focus on Jesus and His kingdom?

3. In what areas have you allowed yourself to feel "entitled" to be self-indulgent in what the world is offering you? Why? What pain might you be trying to mask or numb? Take time to confess this to your heavenly Father now and ask for His healing and grace.

4. Take assessment of the *right* and the *wrong* in the way you relate to your family. In what areas are your family choices holy? In what areas are they not?

5. Take assessment of the *good* and the *better* in the way you relate to your family. What "good" things might you need to set aside so that the "better" can allow you and your family to thrive spiritually?

6. In what areas do you need wisdom to hear God's voice today? Prayerfully ask your heavenly Father to pour out His wisdom on you to discern His voice over the Enemy's, and to give you courage to do what He asks.

4

Free Indeed

For the I-Can't-Say-No Parent

---

*What a curious phenomenon it is that you can get men to die for
the liberty of the world who will not make the little sacrifice that
is needed to free themselves from their own individual bondage.*

Bruce Barton, *It's a Good Old World*

In C. S. Lewis's book *The Lion, the Witch and the Wardrobe*, the author describes the plight of Edmund, a young man who finds himself in prison. He thought he was going to receive an endless supply of his favorite candy, Turkish Delight, but instead he has nothing to eat and is bound in a cold, dark dungeon.

When I think, with eyes of freedom, of my life and the lives of my family members, I recognize how truly bound we are by this world. We are slaves to our smartphones, our jobs, making more money, being more successful, and looking more youthful. Our children are slaves to peer pressure, cultural and societal norms, and their feelings of inadequacy and loneliness in an era when they are more "connected" than any generation that has preceded them.

A friend of mine once noted that social media, with all the good it can offer, also paints a competitive culture for youth where they feel as though they are comparing their mundane life with the "highlight reel" of someone else's. Young people are tempted to assess the value of their looks, experiences, and achievements by how many "likes" they receive on any given post. Often, I-Can't-Say-No parents feel sorry for their children and want to make life easier for them, or they simply can't say no for fear of being rejected and alone. Either way, this type of family dysfunction enables children to become stuck in destructive or childish behaviors and so brings bondage for all family members.

When psychologists use the term "enabling," they mean helping (through action or lack of action) a person to indulge in destructive behaviors. Parents don't mean to enable their children to do things that will ultimately harm the children, but sometimes pity or fear of rejection tempts a parent to do just that.

Enabling Behaviors

Let's take a quick assessment. As you think of your relationship with your children (or child), how many of these categories are you guilty of?

- Repeatedly bailing them out of "tight spots" they get themselves into

- Giving them "one more chance," then another … and another
- Ignoring the problem because they get defensive when you bring it up or because you are hoping it will magically go away
- Joining them in blaming others for their own feelings, problems, and misfortunes
- Avoiding problems—keeping the peace, believing a lack of conflict will help
- Doing for them what they should be doing for themselves, such as chores or other responsibilities
- Softening or removing the natural consequences of problematic behavior
- Trying to "fix" them or their problem
- Trying to control them or their problem[1]

Psychotherapist Don Carter states:

Enabling behavior is born out of our instinct for love. It's only natural to want to help someone we love, but when it comes to certain problems—helping is like throwing a match on a pool of gas.

In the true sense of the word, to enable is *to supply with the means, knowledge, or opportunity to be or do something—to make feasible or possible.*

In its true form, then, Enabling behavior means something positive. It's our natural instinct to reach

out and help someone we love when they are down
or having problems.

However, when we apply it to certain problems
in living … *enabling behaviors have the reverse effect
of what is intended.*[2]

In becoming a Spiritually Healthy parent, you will need to assess
your current ways of dealing with difficult situations, and determine
if you are helping or hurting in the way that you respond. The "helping" responses breed freedom, while the "hurting" responses breed
bondage.

The Witch Is Gone

I wonder how often we choose to *not live* in freedom. Not live the
abundant life that Jesus has promised. In Christ, the witch is gone,
the chains are broken—and yet we cower away in our prison cells,
starving, afraid, and alone.

Isaiah 42:7 declares that Jesus came to open blind eyes, free cap-
tives from prison, and release those who sit in darkness from the
dungeon. In order to be truly free, I must answer these questions: In
what ways am I blind? To whom am I a captive? Where do I sit in
darkness? Essentially, what am I enslaved to?

Jesus said, "So if the Son sets you free, you will be free
indeed" (John 8:36). What did Jesus mean when He said these
words, and what impact does this freedom have on our lives and
our children's lives? Let's first back up a few verses to where Jesus
said in John 8:31–32, "If you hold to my teaching, you are really

my disciples. Then you will know the truth, and the truth will set you free."

Truth is, by definition, objectively true regardless of any consideration. Our very real Enemy, Satan, will continually try to sabotage this by making us feel or think that truth is relative to our situation or pain. Isn't it amazing how quickly we can justify incorrect thinking based on our circumstances? I find myself doing it all the time. It's one thing to believe something until it stands in the way of security or personal gain.

When we are willing to declare truth as truth, *no matter what*, we begin to understand freedom.

Truth and Freedom

I believe that at the root of an I-Can't-Say-No parent is a broken person who, at some level, has not clearly understood what is true.

Here's an example: God is good. This is true. Goodness is His character. The Bible and God Himself say this is truth. However, consider a young man who has known nothing but abuse from his parents and poverty and injustice from the world. He lives in isolation from others. To say to this man "God is good" would fall on deaf ears because his experience tells him otherwise.

To this man, God is not only "not good," but He is also not just, near, or loving. His experience *interprets his view* of God (what is true) rather than *truth being used to interpret his experience*. We may say, "Well, *his truth* is that God is not good." What we mean when we say "his truth" is something that is a critical concern for young people today. Truth is now relative to a situation or an experience, and to think otherwise is to be thought of as ignorant or intolerant. This is the type of thinking that our children are being influenced by every day!

The Cost of Living on Script

As we begin to "live on script" and submit to what God is doing in each of our lives, please know that the Enemy will begin to seduce us—and our children.

He will offer each of us a multitude of counterfeit identities. He will lie to us, deceive us, and rob each of us of our true identities if he can. He wants nothing more than to destroy our families. Look around. Look at the pain and the deceit in families today. Look at marriages falling apart as quickly as they are being joined together. Look at how "Until death do us part" really only means "until I find someone more compatible" or "until I can't stand living with you anymore."

Peter states that "your enemy the devil prowls around like a roaring lion looking for someone to devour" (1 Pet. 5:8). Our marriages and our children are both at war. We are on a true battlefield, and our Enemy is real. Sometimes we think the way to battle this is to say yes and to give in to every indulgence that our children demand.

As a parent, I lose sight of *this* Enemy at times. I lose sight that the real Enemy of my children's hearts and souls is a powerful evil that preys on them, and on my life and marriage as well. With trickery and distortion, he promises everything and gives nothing but pain, regret, and bondage. I may think that I'm giving my child everything she wants, but in reality I'm robbing her of freedom.

It is interesting to me that the apostle Paul began his letter to the church in Ephesus with his readers' identity in Christ, but he ended in chapter 6 with the realization that Satan will seek not only to thwart that identity but *destroy it*.

> Finally, be strong in the Lord and in his mighty power. Put on the full armor of God, so that you can take your stand against the devil's schemes. For our struggle is not against flesh and blood, but against the rulers, against the authorities, against the powers of this dark world and against the spiritual forces of evil in the heavenly realms. (Eph. 6:10–12)

Paul knew as assuredly as Christ came to give us His truth and His character that Satan would come to steal that from us. The Bible tells us that our Enemy, the Devil, began his treachery against mankind in the garden by deceiving Eve, and that his final act in this world will be when he is unleashed to deceive the nations. His favorite tool is *deception*.

Being Deceived

So what is the alternative? Simply start saying no to more? No to our children—just to show them who is boss? No to our spouses—just to stand up for our positions and plans?

It's really not so much about the amount of yeses or nos; it's *about the brokenness behind our answers*.

Let me give you an example of this brokenness from my own marriage. My husband and I have gone through some very real struggles in the past few years. We moved away from our hometown of over twenty years for my husband to take a new position in a new career. Honestly, I wasn't a fan of the decision. I struggled to be supportive of our new life. I resented having to leave my family, home, friends, and job. Inside, the no in my heart was out of resentment and pain, and this resentment created a crack in my spiritual armor for Satan to begin his deception.

My new job and my husband's new job were more demanding than we realized. Our schedules and travel kept us away from each other for weeks at a time. I also suffered a horrible accident shortly after our transition and was in recovery. This recovery and the medical attention I needed had to be done five hours away from where my husband had to be for his work. Again, more resentment crept into my heart as I endured this challenge largely away from the comfort of our marriage.

My husband was also feeling neglected. I wasn't there to help him in his new responsibilities and offer the support that I had given as his wife for almost twenty-three years.

Trying to be brave, we put our heads down and tried to get through it. I think we didn't really try to get help or wisdom from God or those around us because, again, we deceived ourselves into thinking that "this too shall pass." If we ignored it, maybe it would just go away.

The Bitter Root

The problem with this idea is that resentment, bitterness, and feelings of neglect rarely just go away on their own. This is why we are cautioned in the Bible to "see to it that no one falls short of the grace of God and that no bitter root grows up to cause trouble and defile many" (Heb. 12:15).

Ah, the dreaded bitter root. At first, bitterness is just that—a root. It's underground and no one can see it. Most of the time we barely know it is there. It lies undetected, storing up energy and strength, waiting for its moment to unleash itself. By the time it forces through the soil and makes itself known, it is fully mature and ready to bear fruit. Yet the fruit of bitterness is no delicacy at all. It is vile in every way.

This is exactly what happened one day in our marriage. Without warning my root made its grand appearance, and neither I nor my husband saw it coming. I had become convinced that we needed some time "to figure things out." This is code for me wanting a little distance. I knew in my heart that I desperately loved and respected my husband, but I was hurting—and the Enemy was whispering to me that time away would stop the hurting. But he is a liar.

Instead, my husband and I wept together. We sat in our living room for six hours just talking, crying, and sharing our hearts. God was present, and His power and love for us was far greater than the power of the grotesque impostor who had been lying to me. His grace met us there in the living room that day. His truth made everything crystal clear to me. It was as if I had been under the influence of something and had now become sober.

I loved my husband deeply, but it wasn't until God showered me with His love that I was able to forgive, receive forgiveness, and join together with my husband, instead of giving up or going away. We decided to make some big changes that day—and God instigated and made some *for us*.

We are no longer going in two different directions but are learning afresh how to be "one" and do every aspect of life together in joy. We just finished celebrating our twenty-sixth wedding anniversary, and are learning to love and respect each other in this new season of life. I can say victoriously and with confidence that God is indeed bigger and more powerful than any crafty scheme of the Enemy when we surrender our bitterness in order to embrace His love.

A Spiritual Battle

Dr. Jim Burns, prolific author and ministry leader, shed this light on spiritual warfare in marriage:

> I don't know about you, but I believe there is a spiritual battle that takes place for the soul of every marriage. Satan opposes spiritual growth in couples for obvious reasons. I can't speak for Satan, but I believe he never hesitates to go for the jugular, which is your marriage. Sure the power of evil brings sin into our lives, but Satan also does something else that is more subtle: He causes a couple to settle for a lack of spiritual intimacy. He knows there is heavenly power against him that can pay dividends for generations to come when a couple walks together spiritually![3]

The Bible is clear: "Greater is he that is in you, than he that is in the world" (1 John 4:4 KJV). And James 4:7–8 gives us the strategy for the winning in this battle: "Submit yourselves ... to God. Resist the devil, and he will flee from you. Come near to God and he will come near to you."

In his book *The Sacred Search*, Gary Thomas points out the reality that so many people are living in when it comes to finding freedom. They don't think of freedom from the bondage of sin. They are only thinking about the emancipation from their marriage. Thomas counsels many spouses who are afraid of what God could do if they allowed Him to. What if God really healed their marriage and they had to stay in it? What they are forgetting is that when God heals, He restores and renews—but our expectations also have to be correct.

Thomas wrote:

> Can I be honest with you? There isn't a person alive who can keep you enthralled for the next five or six decades. If they're really funny, really attractive, and you're really infatuated, you can be enthralled for a few years, but selfish people—even wealthy selfish people, or beautiful selfish people, or famous selfish people—eventually get bored with each other, and the very relationship that once gave them security and life feels like prison and death. No matter how intensely you feel in love now, the same thing will happen to you if you get married without a shared mission.[4]

The Sacred Search calls for people who are thinking about getting married (or are already married) to align their focus on the "why" of marriage instead of the "who." In the why, we find ourselves on a mission together, and this transcends some of the petty things we find ourselves complaining and bickering about.

Freedom Defined

So whether you are the parent or spouse who embodies the I-Can't-Say-No profile because you *want to be loved,* and you find identity in enabling others (in a codependent kind of way), or your heart says no because your family *should be loving you better,* either way your heart cries out to be loved. We want love and we want it freely given. We don't want to have to earn it, because then it doesn't feel like love; it feels like payment.

There are two kinds of freedom, spiritually speaking. One is positional; the other is functional. On the one hand, to be free is to be set at liberty from the domain of sin. Biblical scholars refer to this as "justification." It means that I am now justified or put right before a holy God for my sin. The penalty for sin was and is paid for by Jesus's death on the cross. He took the punishment in my place. So *positionally* I am free from sin. Why? Because God loves me. He really loves me.

But there is another kind of freedom. It's the practical one that I live in every day. It raises the question, "Am I *functionally* free?"

When I was growing that root of bitterness in my heart, nothing changed about my position in Christ. I was still positionally free. I was still His child. My life and my future were secure in His love and grace. But practically speaking, I was not free. I was functioning out of a place of bondage to my lack of forgiveness and my entitlement to hold bitterness against my husband. I wasn't actively choosing this bondage; it simply became that vile fruit that we discussed earlier.

For the I-Can't-Say-No parent, we who are in Christ and have received His gift of love and forgiveness are positionally free. No matter how we seek to fill our need for others to love us, it doesn't change this. However, practically we are not free. We cannot truly be free when we choose to run around looking for our children and others to fill our need to be loved. This dysfunction creates a bondage that takes us further away from love—not closer to it.

Remember the verse we looked at earlier: "So if the Son sets you free, you will be free indeed" (John 8:36)? This is the only way to true freedom, both positionally and functionally. I don't know about you, but one without the other doesn't make much sense to me! And life without God's love would create in us a vacuum that is insatiable.

What Makes Us Free

In Romans 11:36, the apostle Paul said, "For from him and through him and for him are all things. To him be the glory forever! Amen."

These words conclude the first eleven chapters in the book of Romans. In those chapters, Paul created an airtight defense of Christ's satisfactory work on the cross over all our sin and the law that condemns us. These chapters tell us what He has done—what has come through Him and has been credited to our accounts because of His final sacrifice. It's incredible!

Then chapter 12 begins,

> Therefore, I urge you, brothers and sisters, in view
> of God's mercy, to offer your bodies as a living sac-
> rifice, holy and pleasing to God—this is your true
> and proper worship.

It's "in view of God's mercy" that we can do anything in life
that is of meaning. It's "in view of God's mercy" that we live and
breathe. It's "in view of God's mercy" that our marriages and our
families can not only stay together but also thrive. Remember, this
is His story and He knows the beginning from the end. We have
been grafted in by grace and given a part to play in His script. And
His grace is sufficient even for the most messed-up families. Praise
God for that!

Young children seem to understand this freedom more than
anyone else. I know of a five-year-old girl who has had painful family
circumstances most of her short life. Yet she knows how to sense
God's mercy, grace, and freedom in the midst of the difficulty. Her
prayers remind me that when we focus on our messed-up circumstances, we feel the need to react out of bondage, but when we focus
on our heavenly Father, we feel we can respond out of freedom.

One night, this little girl's grandmother ("Mimi") recorded one
of her prayers. This is what she prayed:

> *Dear Jesus,*
> *Thank You for Mimi; I love her so much. I think*
> *that all that You have made is the best. Please don't ever*

*take my Mimi away—I love her so, so much. She's the
bestest ever. Thank You for my brother; he is the bestest
too. Thank You for all my friends too—because those are
the best people in my life. You don't have to make it any
special-er. Because what You do for me is so great.*

*What can we do for Your people? We really want
to do something for Your people. I really want to do
something for You. And, for people who don't have
food, beds, homes, and all kinds of stuff like that. I
love everyone. And I love You just the way You are.*

*And, I'm so happy that you are our King. Nobody
else is our King. You are our King. You are the Lord
over all angels. The Devil is bad, and You are good.
Thank You for everything You made, and we love You
so, so much—and nothing can defeat You.*

You are the bestest ever.

In Jesus's name, Amen.

"You are our King"? "Nothing can defeat You"? Really? Wow,
I wonder what my faith and freedom would be if I began to pray
more like a five-year-old? In her little life she already has reason to
be in bondage from life's ill circumstances, but her father and her
grandmother are choosing to model mercy and grace to her.

I believe God is victorious and that this will be her prayer when
she is fifty as well. We can take a lesson from a child. We can no
longer choose to hold onto our hurts and the offenses done to us
when we have received such lavish grace and forgiveness from our
heavenly Father.

Not Receiving What We Deserve

Grace and love go hand in hand. Until we really experience grace, we will find it hard to receive God's love. And until we receive God's love, we will seek love by dysfunctionally trying to win it from others.

At the heart of the gospel (which literally means "good news") is the idea of grace and mercy. Some have said that grace is receiving what you don't deserve, but mercy is *not* receiving what you *do* deserve. Have you ever not received a consequence you were due, and at the same time also were given something good that you weren't due? It's in this combination that we experience the fullness of God's love. Because of His great love for us, He showed mercy (not giving us the punishment of sin which we deserved—death—see Romans 3:23) and then lavished us with *grace* (adopting us as His beloved children, giving us His Spirit, and making us heirs to an eternal inheritance—see Ephesians 1:2–14).

Our Response

We have been given the freedom from the bondage of sin *and* the presence of God, now and for eternity! What is the appropriate response to such a gift? Paul told us that the reasonable response would be to offer up our lives as living sacrifices (see Rom. 12:1). When I think about a sacrifice, I think of something that is dead. But Paul indicated that we are living sacrifices. That is an oxymoron, isn't it? Yet, we are both. We are alive in Christ and dead to sin and bondage. We are dead and yet we live.

Paul said in another one of his letters,

> I have been crucified with Christ and I no longer
> live, but Christ lives in me. The life I now live in the
> body, I live by faith in the Son of God, who loved
> me and gave himself for me. (Gal. 2:20)

So we died because of sin, but now Christ gives us a new life to play a part in His story on His terms. He is the Director, and He calls the shots. I may not like the scene or the setting, but He is first in charge. This is our only response. This response is our worship to a God who loves us.

Saved for Something

There is a scene in the movie *Les Misérables* where a convicted criminal steals silver housewares from the home where a bishop gave him a place to rest and eat for the night. When caught by the authorities, he is brought to the bishop to be held accountable. Upon seeing the man in his desperation, the bishop announces to the police that those silver items were a gift and that they belong to the criminal.

When the police leave, the gentle bishop reminds this man that his newfound freedom is not in vain, but rather he had been "*saved for the Lord.*"

I believe that we often see ourselves saved *from* sin and forget that we have also been saved *for* something. There is the freedom from sin so *that* we can now live abundant lives in this world—in our families. The "something" that we do with our freedom is of extreme importance for our marriages and in raising our children.

One Woman's Story

Fear keeps the I-Can't-Say-No parent in bondage, because if she does say no, someone might abandon, mistreat, or not love her. She can't afford for this to happen, so she lives in the bondage of people-pleasing—and this includes her children.

I know of a wife and mother who was starving herself to ensure that her husband would find her attractive (and not have an affair). She was also spreading herself too thin working for the school board, volunteering in her child's classroom, and being a team mom for her kids' sports in order to show the world she was an engaged and good mother. Meanwhile she was working part-time as an interior designer, trying to make her clients happy even at the loss of her own time or income. Demands from her friends and her aging parents added another level of performance and bondage.

When I met her, she was in denial about this being an unhealthy way to live. She argued that everyone was happy, so she must be doing a good job. I asked her if she was happy and living the abundant life that God intended for her. With that she broke down in tears. One question and this seemingly superwoman crumbled. She confessed that she was using drugs and alcohol to manage depression and her weight. She was engaged in an emotional affair, which gave her an outlet where someone seemed to appreciate her without asking for something in return. Underneath the surface she was coping with her pain in dysfunctional ways.

As I began counseling with her, I realized that her situation was both emotional and spiritual. It was emotional because she was a woman who feared failure and abandonment, and it was spiritual because she had never come to the place of truly believing and receiving that God would never abandon her. She did not believe there was nothing she could do to either earn or lose God's love.

In many ways, so many of us are like this woman. It seems just too good to be true. But it is. Scripture makes it clear that we did (or could do) *nothing* to earn God's love. Our greatest acts are still nothing more that filthy rags before God (see Isa. 64:6). Once we accept that we can do nothing to earn this gift, it is easier to understand not being able to lose it.

God's Word is meant to give us truth about who God is and our relationship to Him, and also to be used to "renew our minds" when the Enemy or society seduces us into believing a lie.

This woman's situation did not change overnight, but as she immersed herself in honest relationships with other Christian women (where she could share her hurts, failures, and fears) and in God's Word through Bible study, she began to feel more empowered to say yes to healthy choices and no to the unhealthy patterns in her life. She began to establish boundaries with her time and energy, with her interactions with the opposite sex, with drugs and alcohol, and with the scarcity of her food intake. Although she would tell you these things are a daily battle, she now wakes up each morning feeling the freedom of living in the abundant (not perfect) life.

What if we woke up every morning declaring our positional freedom in Christ and chose this freedom in every difficult relationship, responsibility, and struggle? What if, by acknowledging and living as if the shackles were really off, we began to understand that our happiness is not dependent upon saying yes to those around us to make them love us, or no to those who have hurt us or failed us, but rather on whether or not we are freely acting out our script *as written*? What if this became the life that we modeled to our children—not running after our happiness, or even theirs, but living in our freedom?

The remedy for the brokenness in the I-Can't-Say-No parent is to receive God's love and the freedom that follows. If not, we will not only receive the bondage of unhealthy relationships, but we will also, over time, see this bondage manifest itself as bad habits and traits, and even as enslavement and addiction. I know this because I am aware of these tendencies in myself, and I see them in those I love.

Lust, alcoholism, drug abuse, pornography, adultery, anger, bitterness, entitlement, selfish ambition, pride, deceit—what might be enslaving you today? God is shouting, "Be free—*free indeed*."

You see, God is the perfect parent. He will never be the yes-only parent. He can and *will* say no, not out of anger toward us, but out of His love for us. Out of His desire to see us healthy and thriving in freedom toward the life He has envisioned for each of us.

Reflect and Respond

1. Consider where you are displaying I-Can't-Say-No tendencies in your relationships. What is at the root of needing to keep peace and have others like you?
2. Ask yourself: Am I positionally free but functionally in bondage? Consider what circumstances and life events have led you to this place.
3. Write out the things that are keeping you from experiencing freedom. Be specific. In what ways am I blind? To whom am

I a captive? Where do I sit in darkness? Essentially, what am I enslaved to? Next, find someone safe to share this list with, and create a plan for implementing healthy boundaries in each category while holding yourself accountable to this person. *Note: Sometimes this is a friend or family member, but sometimes hiring a professional counselor is helpful too.*

4. What does the Bible declare about God and His character? Consider who He is in this moment, separating your thoughts from the things that you may or may not have experienced in this world.

5. We are called to offer our lives back to God for His use as a response to the mercy and grace that has been shown to us. In what ways can you practically put this into action this week in your family?

6. Do you have a "root of bitterness" growing up inside you about anyone in your family? If so, who? Confess this to God, and seek restoration and healing. Consider what it would look like to spend some time with this family member to discuss this rather than distancing yourself.

7. Pray a prayer of victory to our King and our Lord. Pray with the boldness of childlike faith, choosing to offer mercy and grace to others as an act of your worship to God.

5

Beyond the Pursuit of Perfection

For the Driver Parent

---

*To live by grace means to acknowledge my whole life story,
the light side and the dark. In admitting my shadow side,
I learn who I am and what God's grace means.*

Brennan Manning, *The Ragamuffin Gospel*

There has been a lot of talk lately about the modern family. So what is a *modern family*? Well, in one sense, *modern* refers to family structure. Families are made up of a variety of circumstances for raising children: single-parent, two-parent, grandparent, blended, adopted, foster, multigenerational, same-sex, and even those who are "spiritual family." In fact, more than one hundred different family structures have been identified in our world today. And just when we think we have a handle on this, the idea of family changes again.

Modern also offers the world to our families. Modern says it can grant our family members more, better, and something that is just plain "sexier" than we currently possess. Modern seems intriguing, innovative, and indulgent. It seems attractive, even when we think we *shouldn't* desire it.

When I think about the word *modern*, I think about something that is new, improved, and tailored for the current conditions of life. In order to be effective at this, I must watch and change with the world.

So how is it possible to be a modern family and also a spiritually healthy family? Are these two things at odds? I mean, must we either have a modern family that is culturally relevant and satisfied or a spiritual family that stays away from the world and those in it, irrelevant and cloistered away where it is safe?

And why do we want to indulge in the world anyway? Isn't God supposed to be *enough*? Why do we find ourselves either secretly or overtly desiring what this world offers us—and our children? This tension, at its core, is not so much about our relationship with the world as much as it is about our *relationship with God*.

Disappointment with God

We chase after the ever-changing world because, quite frankly, many of us are disappointed with God.

Yep, I said it.

Disappointed. With. God.

If we are honest, we have to say that at some point we have felt this. We look at our mates, our kids, our jobs, our bodies, our financial portfolios, our statuses, our singleness, our health, our houses, or our cars—and we each think, *I saw this playing out differently.*

At some point maybe we said yes to following Jesus and giving our entire lives to Him to do with as He pleased. But somewhere along the way, we took assessment and wondered if that was such a good idea after all. Why should we give up the reins to our individual lives and the lives of our family members? Something deep inside makes us doubt.

With doubt comes fear.

With fear comes isolation.

Then the "world" steps in and offers companionship. And because we are lonely, we take the bait.

The Grand Intersection

When we take the bait, we do one of two things: we either strive for a "modern" approach to family—buying up, saving up, and even giving up—or we come to our senses, recognizing the futility of striving, and we "offer up" our lives to God and to our family members.

At the core of this grand intersection of life is the answer to what we have done with our disappointments.

I truly believe that God uses family to help us reconcile this struggle that is within us. Make no mistake about it—this is a spiritual struggle and none other. Our family members literally *exploit* our sinfulness.

The close proximity in which we live with them extracts the essence of everything carnal that is in us. We see who we truly are and what we demand from God both verbally and silently. And ironically, it is in this very condition that we see our *need* for God as well.

Redeeming Imperfections

You see, we really do need Him. We are literally lost without Him. If we strive after things to comfort our disappointments, we are proclaiming that we don't need God or His script. We choose to rebel against His plotline and script our own.

But when we admit our imperfections and disappointments and submit to His plan, we become servants of His to fulfill His will—not our own.

So do we have disappointments in life, in our family members, in ourselves? Yes, we do. But our families are being used to draw us to our heavenly Father, a Father who does not disappoint.

God our Father is perfect and redeems our imperfections, failures, and disappointments to reveal Himself. He is the "something more" that our hearts long for. And if we allow it, our families, because of (not in spite of) disappointments, will become the catalysts for finding the more that we were really created for in the first place.

So, take a moment right now as you read this chapter to thank God for your family, imperfections and all.

Thank God for your disappointments.

"Give thanks in all circumstances" is the instruction given to us in 1 Thessalonians 5:18. Because ultimately, He knows what is for our good and His glory. In admitting this, we can stop trying to "make it better" with our drive to achieve, and receive grace to accept the things we cannot change.

A Life-Sized Mirror

Our children are like full-length, life-sized, animated mirrors. Their lives, behaviors, and choices mimic who we are. They behave like us, repeat our words and voice inflections, and value what we value. They are a real-time report card of who we are—not necessarily who we want to be.

When my son was in preschool, he drew a picture for me on the front of a homemade Mother's Day card. The picture of me was a simplistic round circle for a head, a big smile, and two bright, shining eyes. I was thrilled that my son viewed me as such a joyful person. Then there was my hair. I had long blonde hair on the sides, but at the top of my head, he had used a black crayon. Curious, I asked my son, "Is Mommy wearing a hat in this picture?" "No," he replied. "Mommy, your hair is yellow here (pointing to the side of my head), but on the top it is black." As busy moms, we can get a few weeks delinquent in taking care of our roots, but *really*? Half of my hair was black!

I smile when I think of his exaggerated perspective. I also realized that day that my son would be a mirror that reflected what I portrayed to others. He would allow me to see what I had never seen before—*if I was willing to look.*

In the Bible, the book of James gives good advice to not only hear what is true, but also do something about it. James said:

> Do not merely listen to the word, and so deceive yourselves. Do what it says. Anyone who listens to the word but does not do what it says is like someone who looks at his face in a mirror and, after looking at himself, goes away and immediately

forgets what he looks like. But whoever looks intently into the perfect law that gives freedom, and continues in it—not forgetting what they have heard, but doing it—they will be blessed in what they do. (James 1:22–25)

One of the most beautiful ways that God will spiritually form us is by using our children to help us see our lives in a spiritual mirror. Yet what we see in our lives will offer us two options: we can lean in to God so He can form us to look more like Jesus, or we can choose to walk away, immediately forgetting what we look like. The second option is tragic.

The Insect and the Buffalo

Then there will be events in life that simply don't make sense to us. When these occur, the Driver parent says, "I will step in and fix it. I will work harder. Achieve more. Whatever it takes, *I will* make it right."

We see this not-making-sense stuff throughout the pages of the Bible as well, an undercurrent that there is often something more to the plotline than the eye can see. We get hints along the way. We have momentary glimpses into people's lives and get the thirty-five-thousand-foot view of what God is doing. We even watch how people respond to this perceived plotline. And sometimes when we read the Bible all the way through, we "get it." It makes sense. We see what God was doing in those times of confusion.

There is a great example of this in the book *The Insect and the Buffalo*. The authors, Roshan Allpress and Andrew Shamy, recount a story of a man from the BaMbuti people who live in the dense forested valleys of the northeastern Congo in Africa. Their way of life is marked by geographical and cultural isolation. The only life they know is a dense rain forest of bushes and trees.

In the 1950s a British anthropologist studying the BaMbuti culture and lifestyle formed a relationship with one of the tribesmen, Kenge, who had never left the confines of the forest. One day the anthropologist took Kenge on a journey miles and miles away from his village. As they entered the plains, Kenge was at a loss for words to describe what he was seeing. Able to see for hundreds of miles, his perception was playing with his mind.

At one point, Kenge asked the anthropologist what kind of insect they were seeing up ahead of them. The way the insects moved was unfamiliar to Kenge. Perplexed, the anthropologist looked on the horizon and saw a herd of buffalo far in the distance but no insects. Then it dawned on him what Kenge was seeing and perceiving. He told Kenge that the "insects" he saw were in fact buffalo, but that they looked smaller because they were so far away.

Like Kenge, we have only known our very small and fallen world. This is our context for how we interpret our lives and even God. We have never been able to leave our "forest," and because of this, we can only perceive what is *so much bigger* and *grander* as something as small and insignificant as an insect.

A Fresh Perspective

This "forest perspective" happens when we read the Bible. As we read an isolated portion or story line in God's Word, we find ourselves utterly perplexed. On the surface of our limited understanding, the Bible is incomprehensible.

Yet as we keep reading through the chapters that span hundreds of years in Scripture, we see *why* God asked Noah to build an ark with his sons—He was going to save them from catastrophe and bless them.

After a long and unjust narrative, we finally understand *why* Joseph was betrayed by his brothers and sent to Egypt as a slave— God was going to spare his family (and the lineage of the Messiah) from famine.

We *make sense* of how Esther, a young Jewish orphan, was placed as queen in the Persian palace—to save her people from death.

We also see the object lessons God desires to teach us through life events that on the surface don't make sense. It's only in retrospect that we begin to understand *why* God conquered Jericho with only trumpet sounds and shouts—so that the army of Israel would know that God was the one who fought their battles. But at the time, don't you think that these soldiers were scratching their heads and saying, "Are you sure about this? I mean, this is a huge city with enormous walls, and I think it may take more than some marching and shouting"?

There's *more clarity* for the reader about Job and his suffering when we know that God was testing his faith and proclaiming to Satan (and all those watching) that His servant's heart was true. But in the midst of his pain and misery, Job had real questions.

In awe, we begin to *understand* the painful sacrificial system found in the Old Testament and how it was setting up *why* Christ would pay for the penalty for our sin by death on the cross. But at the time, the God-fearing people of the Old Testament were burdened with sacrifices, and later Jesus's mother and the disciples mourned profusely as they buried their hope in redemption when Jesus was on the cross.

On *this* side of things, the story makes more sense. In the *midst of it, however,* it really doesn't make any sense at all.

The Upper and Lower Story Lines

Randy Frazee, author of *The Heart of the Story*, said:

> To better understand [the Bible], we will need to view it with a dual lens.... [The] individual stories from the Bible ... [are] our Lower Story.
>
> The Lower Story reveals the here and now of daily life, the experiences and circumstances we see here on earth....
>
> But [God] has a higher agenda than our survival and comfort.... The Bible isn't filled with a thousand individual stories of God's intervention just to get people through rough times, but rather one grand story of something larger, something eternal.
>
> This is the Upper Story.[1]

This Upper Story is the lens through which we must train our eyes to view our lives and the lives of our family members. For the Driver parents especially, this requires faith, because we will not have the vantage point of reading our life stories over a period of decades, centuries, or even a millennium. We see our lives today—and often recall our yesterdays—but only God can see our tomorrows.

The Mire or the Blessing

Because of this inability to see from the beginning to the end, we find ourselves caught in the mire of the Lower Story, while God is calling us to see beyond the here and now, with eyes toward redemption, to a "faith future." There's danger in seeing our lives only from the Lower Story. We miss what God is doing in the long run to glorify Himself; we get discouraged; we feel the entire weight of decisions and circumstances on our shoulders; and we begin to lose hope.

Sometimes the mire is excruciating: a debilitating disease, a divorce, the loss of a beloved family member, a financial disaster, or an abuse that has been suffered. Any of these can make us question if God really is indeed good and perfect. When we doubt His goodness and perfection, we want to pursue that perfection for ourselves. The Driver parent is seduced by the pursuit of excellence and "better" at any cost. This mind-set, in his or her opinion, will produce success.

But what about the blessings that come from living in an Upper Story perspective? Is it possible that this perspective could give us a sense of awe in God and those around us? Is it crazy to believe that our focus set on God could bring glory to Him in all circumstances and grace to deal with the imperfections of life and others—even ourselves?

Perhaps this belief is crazy. But it is crazier *not to believe.*

One thing that I have found to be true over and over again is that God delights in using simple, common, and broken people to reveal His power and grace. Did you catch that? Because if we don't catch this, then we will continue to strive toward perfection and force those we love to do so as well.

The truth is that He uses our brokenness.

He uses our disappointments, our commonness.

He uses our simplicity in order to broadcast His supremacy and divinity.

He can use me to impact history—spiritually and eternally—in a way that no one else and no other opportunity on this planet can offer me. When we (and our family members) understand this, we begin to live life as God intended. We stop driving ourselves and family members toward all that this world has to offer, and we start striving for more understanding of what God is up to and how we can play a part in it—aligning our efforts with His.

An Unconditional Promise

Just in case Driver parents (as well as any others) doubt this is true, let me take you on a journey through the mountain peaks in the book of Genesis. This important story line corrected some of my own erroneous thinking a few years back as I listened to Pastor Scott Treadway from Rancho Community Church in Temecula, California, talk about how God deals with those of us who desire to be in the driver's seat.

Let's start with Abram. God made an unconditional covenant with Abram (who became Abraham), saying, "All peoples on earth will be blessed through you" (Gen. 12:1–3). It was God's intention, from the very moment of humanity's sinful fall through Adam and Eve, to redeem us. God made a promise to Abraham that would be unconditionally fulfilled regardless of the actions of mankind to thwart it.

Whew! We are only a few pages into this story line and already I am relieved that this plan is not contingent upon anyone's actions.

Because we would have failed. Period.

God is unconditionally dedicated to accomplish His good plan despite any efforts on our part to destroy it. But, what is this "good plan"? His good plan (or good news) is that God would offer relentless grace to redeem us to a right relationship with Him.

No matter what.

It's the "no matter what" that gets me every time. Really? No matter what? Have you seen my rap sheet? I can't help but love the "no matter what" clause in this agreement. It's unbelievable to me sometimes, but I'm grateful it is there.

In fact, it is a really good thing that this clause is there, because it wasn't long before the plan was doubted. You see, God promised Abraham and Sarah that they would have a son (even late in their years) in whom the redemption and blessing of all the nations would be found. After waiting for God to make good on His promise, they began to doubt. In their doubt they began to fear that God would not do as He said. So they isolated themselves from His plan and took matters into their own hands.

Helping God Out

In some ways, I empathize with them. I mean, in *retrospect*, we see that God fulfilled His promise eventually. But He did take twenty-five

years to do so! Twenty-five years is a long time to remain trusting
and faithful, wouldn't you agree? I get frustrated when I don't see
God take action in response to my prayers within in a week—
sometimes even a day!

Sarah had her husband, Abraham, impregnate her maidser-
vant, Hagar, in order to give him a son. They were trying to "help
God out."

Sound familiar? This is the poster child for the Driver parent. Abraham and Sarah essentially said, "God, we believe You
about what You are ultimately doing, but we sense that You are
not making things happen according to our timetable and in our
way, so we are willing to step in and do our part to help You
accomplish this."

I see this attitude in myself. I see that I am walking in faith
for the "*big picture*," but I'm unhappy with this lower narrative
I'm caught in. I try to step in and alleviate my pain, or the pain
of my child, and delude myself into thinking *I am partnering with
God*. I'm just helping Him out a bit. How sad.

The result of this plan in the story line of the Bible was the
son Ishmael. God did not despise him, but Ishmael was not the
original plan. The original plan was Isaac. And twenty-five years
after the promise from God, Isaac was born to Abraham and
Sarah. Isaac became the son of blessing, yet he was the second
born. In the ancient Eastern culture, that wasn't how things were
done. The firstborn was supposed to receive the blessing and the
inheritance. In giving the blessing to Isaac, God seems to be making the point that He will accomplish His perfect plans in His
ways—not ours.

The Debacle of the Second-Born

In the very next generation, Isaac's son Jacob struggled for the blessing of the firstborn. Jacob was a twin and second to be born. He was the "usurper" who came out grasping the heel of his brother, Esau (see Gen. 25:20–34; 27:36). To "usurp" means "to seize and hold (a position, office, power, etc.) by force or without legal right."[2]

Jacob's mother, Rebekah, who appears to have been a Driver parent, conspired deceit against Isaac to trick him into giving Jacob the blessing instead of Esau—and it worked. She pushed her son to become a lying, deceitful thief in order to climb to the "success" of the birthright. It was success gained, however, at any and all cost.

Again the second born received the birthright. The covenant of grace passed into Jacob's hands. We do know from Romans 9:11–12 that God chose Jacob as heir: "Yet, before the twins were born or had done anything good or bad—in order that God's purpose in election might stand: not by works but by him who calls—she was told, 'The older will serve the younger.'" In Romans 9:16 Paul said, "It does not, therefore, depend on human desire or effort, but on God's mercy."

We get the sobering point that God is making here: *redemption does not depend on us, and we can also do nothing to impede its success.*

My "aha" thus far in the story line is that family brokenness doesn't thwart God's plan.

If this isn't good news, I don't know what is! Family brokenness is all around us. We see lies, anger, and selfishness in today's families. We hear of and witness the misuse of sexuality, money, and power—all to simply get ahead of the other guy. Lives are irrevocably changed in an instant because of drunkenness, despair, and deceit. The fact is that bad news is everywhere, from our own homes to the evening news.

But guess what? When the bad news gets worse, the good news simply gets "gooder." The good news is that Jesus came to seek and save the lost. He has already been found victor over sin and death. In Him, we will one day say good-bye to the pain of this world and enjoy His goodness forever.

I'm a Little Confused

You might be saying to yourself, "I'm a little confused; this story doesn't make sense to me." But maybe this world isn't supposed to makes sense. Maybe God actually uses our brokenness and sin, rather than our clean stories, to accomplish His purposes.

So that's it? We just choose to be okay with all the messiness because we have hope that God is using it? Well, that's part of it— but God graciously seems to allow for *something* more.

Fast-forward in the story line to Genesis 32. Jacob is old at this point. He had dealt with the consequences of his decisions. He was separated from his family, deceived by his uncle, forced to keep running and hiding. Jacob was in his nineties when he received word that Esau was coming after him. Esau was wealthy and had four hundred men with him. Surprisingly, Jacob seemed to say, "I'm going to stop running and face this."

But he also wanted to be in the driver's seat of his circumstances. I've been there—haven't you? Trying to control an *uncontrollable situation.*

He split his group, sending half of his family and wealth in one direction and the other half in another. Then something, rare at this point in Scripture, happened. He prayed.

Jacob's Prayer

Jacob was desperate as he called out to God. Read his prayer in Genesis 32:9–12:

> Then Jacob prayed, "O God of my father Abraham, God of my father Isaac, LORD, you who said to me, 'Go back to your country and your relatives, and I will make you prosper,' I am unworthy of all the kindness and faithfulness you have shown your servant. I had only my staff when I crossed this Jordan, but now I have become two camps. Save me, I pray, from the hand of my brother Esau, for I am afraid he will come and attack me, and also the mothers with their children. But you have said, 'I will surely make you prosper and will make your descendants like the sand of the sea, which cannot be counted.'"

Regardless of whether or not Jacob found favor with his brother, Esau, on that fateful day, God's plan to redeem mankind would be carried out through one of Jacob's sons—Judah. Maybe Jacob's prayer would be answered according to his desires, but maybe not. Either way, the Upper Story plans that God set in action would still be accomplished. The entire lineage is recorded in Matthew 1:1–17.

If you have ever thought of genealogies in the Bible as boring, I encourage you to read this one again with a new set of eyes. Read it with the understanding that regardless of the imperfections of human circumstances and choices, God's perfect plan is prevailing all around us.

Wrestling with God

After Jacob's prayer, he put his plan in action, sending his family and possessions away. Jacob was alone. He spent the night "wrestling" with God. An unusual part of the Bible for sure, but let's not get caught up in the imagery. Instead, let's glean from what it tells us. It's as if God is giving permission to struggle. He says, "Let's wrestle it out. I'll get in it *with* you."

We wrestle with Him, His choices, what He allows—don't we?

There are times in my life and in the lives of my children when painful situations seem overwhelming. I just want to rescue those I love or be rescued myself. I find myself wanting to distance myself from God, because I feel somehow betrayed. Yet the distancing brings only more doubt and more fear—and more pain. Instead, I think God uses this part of the Bible to remind us to stay close to Him.

This passage paints a picture of moments alone with God when we get to *strive with Him*. We often think of it as *negative* to wrestle, to strive. But Jacob was blessed after it and was changed because of it (see Gen. 32:29).

The Driver parent will wrestle with God, but God will prevail. He will win. Of course. But, think about it: we have a God who is willing to wrestle it out with us—no matter what.

At the end of the wrestling with this man-face of God, Jacob was renamed Israel, which means, "One who strives with God." The Messiah (or Savior) came from Israel.

Redemption came from Israel.

Redemption comes from "one who strives with God."

Let's get personal with this for a moment. What in your family, in your life, needs to be wrestled out with God? Disappointment, depression, hurt, shame, fear? What if, instead of hiding from God or trying to figure out things all on our own, we chose to wrestle things out with God? What if we knew that He would "get in it with us" and not shun us for our imperfections, hurt, and despair?

What if we knew that we would encounter Him face-to-face and that He would show us who He is? What if we would be blessed and changed because of our encounters? I think that we, and our families, often miss out on getting honest with God because we are striving so hard to make things better and achieve perfection without Him.

Limps and All

Then Jacob walked forward, limping, to Esau.

As the wrestling match came to an end, Jacob's hip was dislocated by his opponent. We are told that as he left, he did so *limping* (see Gen. 32: 31). We all have limps, don't we? And while we may not feel that these limps are the things that we necessarily want our spouses or our children to see, how can these limps be part of putting the good news of God on display for all to see?

In Genesis 33:4, we see a beautiful picture of redemption for Jacob after he spent his life running from God and others. As Jacob saw Esau, he approached him in humility. "But Esau ran to meet Jacob and embraced him; he threw his arms around his neck and kissed him. And they wept."

If we learn anything from this snapshot of Jacob's story, it is that God uses and heals imperfect people and families who (limps and all) pursue a perfect God together. When we find ourselves being the Driver parents, trying hard to create the perfect families, maybe God is simply calling us to *more*.

Maybe becoming a spiritually healthy family is not about becoming a perfect family but rather following a perfect God together. And in doing so, to find peace with Him, our pasts, and our family members.

Reflect and Respond

1. Prayerfully consider what disappointments you have, either in God or in your life. What are these things? How have these disappointments caused you to look elsewhere to meet your needs?

2. In what ways have your children (or your spouse) acted as mirrors to disclose both attractive and unattractive qualities in yourself or your actions?

3. Can you identify a time when you wanted to "help God out"? Is there a time when you were driving the situation to rescue yourself or someone you love from an unbearable situation and in doing so lost faith in God?

4. When have you believed the lie that your brokenness or the brokenness of your family may eliminate you from participating in the story that God is writing? Are you willing to stop "driving"

and lay down your brokenness and your family in order to receive God's forgiveness and redemption?

5. In what areas may you need to wrestle it out with God? What are some things causing you distress and even distance in your relationship with God? Are you willing to get "in it" with Him and allow His blessing to follow?

6

Relinquishing Control

For the Micro-Managing Parent

I gave in, and admitted that God was God.
C. S. Lewis

We are prone to worry, prone to place the wrong value on things, and prone to have little faith. We are also prone to worship an idol in this human condition. This idol is tantalizing because it gives us a false sense of security—and we take the bait. *We take control.* Control becomes our idol. I'm not talking about merely taking control of our own lives; we also long to manage and control the lives of those around us.

We look around and it seems that everyone else is somehow doing this life thing *better than us* or has *more* than we do. We desire to have more control to ensure that we will not come up short in the end.

Dennis DeYoung, lead vocalist for the band Styx, called it all a "grand illusion," and penned these words decades ago:

> *So if you think your life is complete confusion*
> *Because your neighbor's got it made*
> *Just remember that it's a grand illusion*
> *And deep inside we're all the same....*
> *We made the grade and still we wonder who ... we are.*

Let's Be Honest

If we are honest, these words unveil the reality deep inside each of our hearts. We don't like feeling vulnerable, needy, or left wanting. We don't like our kids being bullied, hurt, or not succeeding in the ways we'd hoped.

We see our brokenness and the brokenness of others around us. All the while, we are seduced into believing that life is somehow better or more abundant for the *other* guy. In the moment we believe that lie, we choose to not serve our Master and live in His kingdom, but to serve another—the master inside ourselves.

Be careful. This master promises *refuge* but gives *bondage* instead.

Controlling Who I Am

Control. Let's face it, who doesn't want to be in charge of his or her life? The final lyrics to the Styx song say that one day we may stop and ask the question, "What is this spell we are under?" We feel under the control of others—whether it's our parents, bosses, spouses, or simply our circumstances of money, popularity, or opportunity. Eventually, this feeling causes us to ask who we truly are. It is a question of identity, and I believe that at the core of our grand illusion is an issue of controlling our identities and the identities of our children. The "spell" that we are under tells us that we can actually take the pen in our hands, write out all the aspects of our lives, and when we do that, finally we will be happy.

This condition of longing for control can have other faces too: self-medicating, escaping, eating disorders, and "guilting" others. We do these things because if power, force, and persuasion don't achieve what we want, we find ways to cope in the meantime. And even these issues can become our way of manipulating others into giving us what we want.

Ouch.

Being honest about ourselves and our motives hurts. But it is an important part of becoming spiritually healthy. We have to get real and call out even the hidden parts of our "acceptable dysfunctions."

I don't normally think of myself as a control freak, but there have been times I have had serious doubts about this. As a parent raising my kids, I can remember those times of feeling the temptation to control things around me. Life gets chaotic. Crazy, busy, expensive—and we drop into bed only to get up and do it all over again. And again.

Someone once said that in raising children, "the days are long, but the years are short."

It's this brevity that causes us to clamp down and take control. The Micro-Managing parent succumbs to the false sense of security that if she deals with her fears and uncertainty by holding on tighter, everything will be okay.

First in Charge

In my book *Spiritual Parenting*, I tell a story about my daughter and me having an epic battle of the wills one day. She was four. As the argument ensued, she announced that she didn't have to obey me because I was only "*third in charge*." She told me that first God was in charge, then Daddy, *then* me. In that moment, although I felt like a failure as a mother, I had a sense of relief, knowing that indeed I was not "first in charge." It wasn't about my parenting perfectly or controlling the behavior or situations of my daughter's life. Instead, that "aha" began a journey for me of discovering how I could come alongside what God was doing in the life of my children, release control, and work *with Him* to accomplish *His plans*.

Think about the myriad of things you want to control right now. Make a list so that this is a real conversation about where you are. Now, consider this idea of taking control and micro-managing the events around you to be nothing more than a "grand illusion."

Intellectually we may know that we are not in control of most of what is important to us, but this doesn't stop us from trying. For example, take this short list:

I am not in control of

- whether or not I or someone in my family gets cancer;
- whether or not the economy crashes;
- whether or not my parents or children get a divorce;

- whether or not war will break out in my country
  or a country that will affect my country's safety or
  soldiers;
- whether or not I am able to get pregnant;
- whether or not I will be in a car accident caused
  by a drunk driver;
- whether or not my company will do layoffs this
  week—and I will be one of them; or
- whether or not a natural disaster will strike my
  home.

This list could go on, but I think we get the point. Most of what is really important, we cannot control. If we believe we can, we are only fooling ourselves. "Don't believe it," Styx sings.

Part of being a spiritually healthy family is to recognize God as first and only in charge. Only He can control the items just mentioned, along with all the things that consume our daily thoughts, such as paying bills, potty training, speech delays, marital conflict, substance abuse, and defiant teenage behavior. When God chooses not to intervene and (in our opinion) "take charge," what is our response?

Do Nothing?

You might be thinking, *Well, because I'm not ultimately in charge, should I just sit back and do nothing?* Not at all. Families today have incredibly difficult (even impossible) decisions to make.

I know of a family who is moving to another state, leaving friends and family behind, in order to have the necessary care for their special-needs daughter that their current home state does not provide. I know of a family who is embattled in court appearances and lawyer affidavits as they fight against extreme bullying at their child's school. Yet another family I know is liquidating all their assets to pay for chemo treatments for the mother of three who is hoping to win her battle against breast cancer.

A close friend of mine had four children. Two were twin girls diagnosed with cystic fibrosis. The daily breathing treatments and back beatings were not the only things that overwhelmed this family. The constant hospitalizations, pursuits to get the girls enough calories, and fears that they might catch a respiratory virus also dominated this family's hours. Yet the other two children had needs as well. There was car pool, homework, laundry, and grocery shopping. But the fight needed to be continued. Every day.

After thirteen years of the family managing all these things, one of the twins lost her battle with this horrible disease. The other family members, and especially the other twin, mourned. But the hard work couldn't cease. A few years later, the living twin needed a lung transplant. The mother was a perfect match. Did she simply give up and do nothing? No, after prayerful consideration she underwent surgery and donated a lung to her daughter.

What she could not control was that the newly donated lung would only buy this girl less than a year.

Those close to the family stood in amazement, watching this family do all they could do, humanly speaking, and then have to relinquish control to their heavenly Father. As each daughter took her last breath on this earth, there were sweet prayers and songs being sung over them. One nurse commented that in her time in that hospital ward, she heard cries from parents that were indescribably painful. She was struck by the peace that was present at this family's bedside in the midst of terrible pain and loss.

Ultimate Control versus Micro-Management

Recognizing God as the one who is ultimately in control of the script of our lives doesn't mean that we do nothing. God is entrusting our children's lives to us as parents. He is asking us to take care of them in an imperfect world. We seldom know all we should or should not do in any given situation, and this is why we need to be in constant and personal communication with God so that we can receive His wisdom.

> But the wisdom that comes from heaven is first of all pure; then peace-loving, considerate, submissive, full of mercy and good fruit, impartial and sincere. (James 3:17)

> For the foolishness of God is wiser than human wisdom, and the weakness of God is stronger than human strength. (1 Cor. 1:25)

One of the best ways to be a good parent to our children is to be a faithful son or daughter to our heavenly Father (because we can't give away something we don't have). When we need to *give away* wisdom, encouragement, strength, and forgiveness to our children, we need to be *receiving* those things from God as well.

Sometimes I think we get so caught up trying to "manage" everything that we forget our need to take some time to simply just "be." *Be with* our heavenly Father in prayer. *Be with* His Spirit as we read His Word. *Be with* our children in their hurt. Be with our spouses in their uncertainty.

In some cultures, when something tragic (such as death, sickness, or other loss) happens, the people in the community show up to simply be with those who are hurting. I think in our modern culture, we often want to respond by doing. "I love the person who is hurting, and so I want to do something to make it go away." It can be anything from our child's dog dying to a mean coach, or an unsuitable teacher—but we just want to do something to fix it, don't we?

Healthy Solutions for Family Members

So what do we do in this tension of doing nothing or micro-managing everything?

One tool that I have found helpful is to remember four steps. These words all begin with *IN* because it's a great reminder to each of us that God wants to "be in it" with us, and He wants us to "be in it" with our family members—but in healthy and helping ways, not overbearing or codependent ways.

We are going to take a look at these four steps that help give a framework to what we can do when we want to create healthy relationships, boundaries, and solutions with family members. Then we will discuss the implications for your family, followed by a practical example to understand what this may look like between a parent and a child (although these steps work well for married couples, siblings, and other family members as well).

4 Steps in Responding to Today's Families
Being "IN" it with them

IN-take (offering listening/love)
- Ask questions
- Withhold judgment
- Cultivate compassion

IN-vestigate (offering counsel)
- Pray/discern: What might God be doing in this situation?
- What does God's Word say?
- What do professionals I trust say?

IN-stigate (offering encouragement and confidence)
- Baby step ... a quick win
- Make it their goal, not yours
- Homework (a conversation, confrontation, confession)

IN-tegrate (offering support)
- Celebrate progress
- Determine next steps
- Who/where will long-term accountability come from for lasting support and sustainability?

Intake

The heart posture for *Intake* is to offer listening and love to your family member. In a world where everyone just wants to say something, listening is a gift. You want to make sure that when you listen, you also give eye contact, undivided attention, and verbal cues to allow your child or spouse to know he is being heard.

After you listen to your family member, ask questions. Doing so will demonstrate that you fully understand what he is sharing. These questions can be asked for clarification or to determine specific feelings about the situation.

What is critical for this step is that your family member feels that he is in a safe and nonjudgmental environment. It's often hard to not look shocked and appalled, but as best as you can, try to listen in love.

And last, prayerfully put yourself in your family member's situation, and ask God to cultivate compassion in your heart to give you a perspective of understanding and empathy.

Investigate

The heart posture for *Investigate* is to receive counsel and then offer it to your family member. As a spiritual parent who is seeking to have a spiritually healthy family, you want to receive counsel from God's perspective first. Praying with and for your child (or other family member) is a powerful way to build your faith together while declaring who is ultimately in control.

You can investigate His Word or receive counsel from your pastor or other Christian friends. In a generation where the world is telling your child that there is no objective truth, you can build her trust in His Word as the best place for finding out what is true and good. It's also important to solicit a professional in the area you are discussing.

Instigate

The posture of the heart for *Instigate* is to offer encouragement and confidence to your child. In this step you want your family member to take a baby step, but that step should be his idea. If he owns it, he is more likely to act upon it.

You can ask questions to help your family member determine what this step should be. But, ultimately, this is where you really want to partner with God's Spirit to have your child or other family member hear from God (not merely your voice telling him what to do). Cheer him on with positive support about his decision to act.

Next you can together determine "homework." This is something that will be followed up on as a result of the baby step that your child has come up with. It should have a due date with the understanding that you will be holding him accountable to his goal.

Keep in mind that often a baby step can be to confront, confess, or simply have a conversation with someone. Sometimes it's about displaying a contrite heart before God.

Integrate

The heart posture for *Integrate* is offering support. This is different from doing it for your child or family member (which, as a parent, I find I often want to do). The Micro-Managing parent wants to rescue, not necessarily come alongside of, in order to empower. After you hold your child accountable to her "homework" from *Instigate*, you want to celebrate her progress. Acknowledge the courage or the faith it took to take action, and then rejoice together.

What will allow this to be more than a onetime act (and actually more spiritually healthy for a lifetime) will be to determine the next steps immediately. Again, you should allow this to be your family member's idea—not yours.

Finally, determine who will hold your family member accountable for the long run. (That person is usually a parent when your children are young, but when they are older, it can be a mentor, teacher, or coach.)

As you finish these steps, it's important to continue to pray with and for your family member.

Getting Practical

Let's get practical with these steps in a real-life parent/child situation. When your children are young, this might take place in a matter of minutes.

1. Perhaps a neighborhood child hits your son, and your son runs in the room to tattle on her. We live in a broken world where we sin and others will sin against us. The reality is that our children cannot control this, and neither can we. What we can do is remember to be "in it" with them. You can stop what you

are doing, get down on his level, and look at him as you listen in love. You offer compassionate words that show empathy, such as, "I'm sure that hurt you, didn't it?" (Intake).

2. Next, you can ask your young son, "What do you think God thinks about what happened?" Let him respond, perhaps noting that what happened would make God upset or sad. Offer what God does want for us, telling your son that He wants us to love and be kind to one another (Investigate).

3. You can then ask what your son thinks he should do about this situation. "What do you think God would want?" Perhaps your son says that God wants us to stop hitting or that God wants him to forgive his friend. Based on the truth that you are able to glean from the conversation, ask your son what he thinks he should do next. He might say, "I'll go back and forgive my friend" or "I'll play nicely" or "I will remind my friend that God wants us to be loving." In these instances, you can offer support and encouragement as he does this action step.

But there will be times when your son may not give an acceptable action step. This is where the Micro-Managing parent gets stuck. When you don't get the answer you want, it reinforces the thought pattern that you indeed need to control your child's every decision and action without taking the time to instruct so that your child could apply a new skill set without you. However, instead of taking control, what you should do is this: When undesirable answers are given, you can ask follow-up questions that guide the conversation to a more compatible resolution. It may take more time, but in the long run, the dividends are worth the effort. Instruct, don't control (Instigate).

4. Follow up with your son to see if he indeed did what he was supposed to. If he did, celebrate with him. If he didn't, you will need to reassign the original task, this time with a consequence for not obeying the first time. Then ask him, "Next time your friend hurts you, what can you do?" Encourage your son to go directly to God in prayer and to his friend for honesty and accountability (Integrate).

Modeling in the Midst of Brokenness

Of course, as our children get older, and when the situation involves multiple people, the steps may be drawn out over weeks or even months. And these steps are in no way magically formulaic. Still, our children need to have this pattern of steps repeated over and over again in their lives for them to understand how to live as broken people in a broken world with other broken people.

Let's face it: I need to have this repeated over and over again in *my* adult relationships. I'm still hurt when a friend or my spouse verbally or emotionally "hits" me. I don't always follow these steps—and I know better.

But we can consistently use this method while modeling it in our relationships with our spouses, friends, or in-laws in order to give us something productive to do with our love rather than controlling or micro-managing every detail.

Our children are watching us, and as we model this type of process, it will become a normal reality for them if they see it working itself out with their family members.

Relinquishing Control

Spiritually healthy families don't cease having brokenness or ugliness in their relationships, but they do begin to approach these things with eyes toward redemption and healing rather than retaliation and becoming the "victim."

You see, when we talk about control, we must identify *why* we feel we need to control even the most microscopic events in our lives. We feel this because of our brokenness and the brokenness of others in our families. When we choose *how* we respond to this brokenness, we can either choose God and His way (surrender) or we can choose ourselves and our methods, means, or manipulations.

When I don't choose God, *I'm choosing dysfunction!*

One of the most important aspects of being a spiritually healthy family or a Spiritually healthy parent—or a spiritually healthy person, for that matter—is that we must *relinquish control.* Unclench those tightly fisted fingers of ours, and with hands wide open before our heavenly Father, say, "Give us this day our daily bread." Just like manna was God's daily bread provision for His people in the wilderness, His daily bread for us is His grace and wisdom—which are wholly sufficient.

We really do have as much grace as we need for today. But it's hard to receive it when our fists are closed.

Reflect and Respond

1. What if you started today—declaring God as *first in charge?* In your life and in the lives of your family members, friends, and colleagues? What if you stopped trying to please them but instead surrendered your fears, failures, and control issues to God Himself? What if you said no to being a Micro-Managing parent and the stress that comes with it, and chose to run straight to God for perspective, comfort, and wisdom? What do you truly think would happen?

2. What is an area of your life that would look radically different today if you were to do the above three things? Discuss this issue in prayer with your heavenly Father. Perhaps begin your prayer with these declarations: *I am not in control—God, You are. I am not now, nor ever will I be, first in charge. God, You are and always will be.*

7

A Time to Bless

For the Criticizing Parent

The single most important concern we should have as parents should be the same primary concern Jesus has for us: We must make it our ultimate goal to help our children know and love God with all their heart. How do we do that? One of the simplest and most powerful ways … is to give them a daily, concrete encounter with His power and favor by laying hands on them and speaking a blessing.

Rolf Garborg, *The Family Blessing*

Think for a moment of something that one of your parents said to you when you were growing up. What is the first thing that comes to mind? Is it positive and edifying? Or does the mere memory of it bring a crippling sting that surprises you on most days?

The Bible tells us that "death and life are in the power of the tongue" (Prov. 18:21 KJV). Our words have the power to crush or heal, to wound or encourage.

Many children often hear cruel statements by a parent during a time of anger, frustration, or insecurity. I recently talked to a friend who heard on multiple occasions growing up, "You were a mistake, you know. I wish you were never born" and "You're really a disappointment to me." These are examples of receiving a verbal *curse*. We all can probably remember at least one from our growing-up years. Isn't it amazing how those words still linger in our minds?

However, many of us have also been the recipients of verbal *blessings* from a parent. And if our parents never blessed us with their words, our heavenly Father offers beautiful words of blessing to each of His children in Christ Jesus.

Before you begin to assess yourself as a parent, before you think of ways that you can bless or stop using your words of criticism for injury, pause for a moment. Pause to hear with new ears the blessings that have been uttered on *your behalf* as truth by God Himself. I encourage you not just to read this list but to engage with every word, allowing God to impress these things on your heart. Take the time to look up each verse and read His words to you.

Blessings from Our Heavenly Father

Child of God. God has adopted me into His beautiful family. I am born of God (Eph. 1:5). I have a new heritage! (1 John 5:1).

Loved. He paid the ultimate price for me (John 3:16).

Forgiven. My God and Father is not dangling my failures in front of me. He has lavished grace upon me (Eph. 1:7).

Seated in heavenly places. Not by any worth of my own, I get to sit in places that I don't deserve (Eph. 2:6).

His workmanship. I haven't arrived, but I am in God's studio as He shapes me into His masterpiece (Eph. 2:10).

Temple of the Holy Spirit. In me abides comfort and teaching. I can know what I need to do or say (1 Cor. 6:19).

Overcomer. I can be victorious in Jesus's name. I don't have to be bound to the ugly things that want to rob me of my inheritance (1 John 4:4; 5:4). I have been raised up in His power and am more than a conqueror! (1 Cor. 6:14).

Prayerful Blessings on Our Behalf

Some of the most powerful words in the Bible for me are blessings that others spoke to the people of God. Here is one of my favorites from the apostle Paul in Ephesians 3:16–21:

I pray that out of his glorious riches he may strengthen you with power through his Spirit in your inner being, so that Christ may dwell in your hearts through faith. And I pray that you, being rooted and established in love, may have power, together with all the Lord's holy people, to grasp how wide and long and high and deep is the love of Christ, and to know this love that surpasses knowledge—that you may be filled to the measure of all the fullness of God.

Now to him who is able to do immeasurably more than all we ask or imagine, according to his power that is at work within us, to him be glory in the church and in Christ Jesus throughout all generations, for ever and ever! Amen.

Categorically Blessed

The Criticizing parent struggles to use his or her words for blessing. Many of these parents fear that their words will create inflated egos in their children or keep them from striving for more, while other parents have never truly had blessings spoken over them and do not know how to use them as verbal gifts.

The book of James in the Bible gives us sound advice about the use of our tongues:

The tongue also is a fire, a world of evil among the parts of the body. It corrupts the whole body, sets

the whole course of one's life on fire, and is itself
set on fire by hell....With the tongue we praise
our Lord and Father, and with it we curse human
beings, who have been made in God's likeness. Out
of the same mouth come praise and cursing. My
brothers and sisters, this should not be. (James 3:6,
9–10)

While there is much power in our words to bless or to destroy,
let's focus on the words that bring blessing. There are many forms
and ways to "speak well" over others. The categories of verbal blessing can include:

Admiration. This is the giving of compliments
or praise about something good that you notice.
For example: "What a beautiful smile." "I like
that you are so helpful." "You're such a wonderful
listener."

Affirmation. This is a specific statement of blessing
intended to encourage someone in what God is
already doing in his or her life. For example: "I see
God giving you His heart for those in need."

Appreciation. This is an expression of gratitude
that something good exists or has happened. For
example: "Thank you for helping me." "I give
thanks to God for providing for us."

Anticipation. This is a blessing for the future. For example: "You're going to bring a lot of people joy today with your loving and caring ways. May the Lord go with you and protect you."

Take some time to consider these four As. How can you practice living these out verbally in your home—choosing to offer blessings in each category to each family member on a regular basis?

A Benediction

An important part of being a spiritually healthy family is in the offering of blessings or "benedictions" to your children. The word *benediction* literally means "good speaking" and is most often translated "blessing."[1]

Numbers 6:22–26 (NKJV) records the Lord instructing Moses to teach Aaron (the high priest) and his sons how to bless the people with these words:

> The LORD bless you and keep you;
> The LORD make his face shine upon you,
> And be gracious to you;
> The LORD lift up His countenance upon you,
> And give you peace.

A simple but very powerful way to counteract being a Critical parent is by inspiring and equipping your children with a daily blessing. A blessing is simply a prayer that you pray over your child that has slightly different language.

Let me explain. In a traditional prayer, we commonly address God directly; for example, "Dear God" or "Dear Jesus." In a blessing, we are speaking directly to the person we are blessing. We can use her name and make sure she knows this blessing is specifically for her.

It can also be a statement that is prayerful in nature but declares truth about God or the life He has called us to, such as, "Grayson, may you know that God's protection and love is always with you," or "James, may you go in His peace."

Scatter like Seeds

It was once said of author F. W. Boreham that he was a man who spent his life "scattering benedictions" when he spoke. It is easy to say we should bless our children, but it has much power when we "scatter" our blessings like seeds, sowing abundantly in every season, and allowing God to use them as He wishes. The children (and other members of our families) who receive our blessings are lifted up in the name of the Lord. This is something God desires for us so much that it is given to us as a *command* throughout the Bible ("bless one another").

A father looks at his son and is delighted to find his own smile, and in the same way, the Lord lifts His face to those made in His own image, shining upon those called the "apple of his eye." The name of the Lord is exalted, we are blessed, and in the blessing, God is glorified. This is the power of the benediction (or blessing).

Jill Carattini said that offering a blessing to another, specifically our children, is a high calling … a mysterious gift given to all made in God's image. The putting of God's name *upon another soul* as we go about life is our tongue's greatest utterance. It is a hopeful command, a most uplifted effort. As God's name is set forth, not only is it God who does the blessing, it is God who is the very fulfillment of the words we offer. *God is the blessing.*

Wow, did you catch that? God is the blessing! To put our children in proximity to God and His character by speaking truth to them allows them to know Him. When they know Him, they can have a genuine relationship with Him.

At the end of Carattini's devotional, she offers a blessing to her readers:

May the blessing of the LORD be upon you, and may you know the joy of putting the name of God upon others. For indeed … blessed are those who rest in the light of God's face.[2]

Practically Speaking

In a world where our children are constantly criticized, I encourage parents to make their blessings to their children *personal* and *intimate*. You can do this by placing your hand on your child's shoulder, head, or arm and looking him or her directly in the eye when you speak. It's always a wonderful time to affirm your love by first telling your child how much you love him or her. After the affirmation of love, speak words of biblical verses or ways that you see God's truth manifesting itself in your child's life.

Example: "Mazie, your mother loves you. You are a child of God, and He has given you His grace and mercy. May your day be filled with opportunities to give that grace to others, and may you seek His best in every situation that comes your way, giving Him the glory in all things."

Whether offered at bedtime or in the morning before everyone leaves for the day, a blessing can be a lifelong gift.

The Blessing

Drs. John Trent and Gary Smalley outlined five biblical steps of giving a blessing to children in their book *The Blessing*: (1) Meaningful Touch, (2) A Spoken Message, (3) Attaching High Value, (4) Picturing a Special Future, and (5) An Active Commitment.[3] I have expanded on these steps below:

> 1. *Meaningful Touch.* Before a word is spoken, there should be the laying on of hands, a hug, or a reaching out to touch. We see this throughout Scripture, both in the Old and New Testaments. Appropriate touch conveys in powerful, nonverbal ways our love and affirmation. Touch prepares the way for our words.
>
> 2. *A Spoken Message.* In biblical times, children weren't left to "fill in the blanks" as to whether they

were valuable to a parent or grandparent. Words were used, aloud and in writing. Today, words can place unconditional love and acceptance into the heart of a child or loved one.

3. *Attaching High Value.* But what words do you say or write? The word *blessing* carries the idea that the person you're blessing is of incredible worth and value, even as an imperfect person. In short, you're helping a child get the picture that you see things in his or her life today, things that make the child special, useful, and of great value to you.

4. *Picturing a Special Future.* With our touch and with our words that attach high value, the response in our children's or loved ones' hearts can be nothing short of *transformational.* The light goes on in their hearts and minds when they realize that because of the way God made them, they can do more than they ever dreamed in living out a God-honoring future.

5. *An Active Commitment.* Blessing children doesn't mean we never discipline them or point out areas where growth is needed. But children know at an incredibly deep level if they have their parents' blessing—if their mom or dad, grandmother, aunt, uncle, or other loved one really sees high value in them—*even during the tough times.* Genuine commitment is an unconditional commitment to an imperfect person that says as long as I have breath,

I'll be there to seek to build these five elements of blessing into your life story.

Formal Times of Blessing

In our children's lives, there are milestones that are highly punctuated when we offer a blessing as a part of the ceremony. Many rites of passages, both inside the church and in life in general, provide opportunities when our children's ears are piqued for listening in ways that often get muffled in the normal routine of life. In chapter 10 we will discuss rites of passage in detail.

One such occasion in my son's life was his graduation from middle school. He was about to enter his high school years, and while he still seemed so innocent to me, I knew that a war would rage for his heart and his allegiance to Christ in the four years that were about to follow.

At a pregraduation ceremony with family and friends, each of us read words of blessing to our children. Here are some of the words that I spoke over my son that day:

Dear Brendon,

It is such an honor for me to be here with you today as your mother. Being your mom has been one of the most significant joys in my entire life. From the moment you were born, you have filled my heart with love and happiness. God gave me the desire of my heart when you were born. Your birth made quite the impact on our family.

You haven't ceased making an impact since that day! With each increasing milestone, it was evident that you were a blessing to everyone you came in contact with. It is fitting that I get to bless you in return today.

You add so much grace to our family. Your sensitive heart has given you insight into situations and people that others at your age may have overlooked. I have never had to ask you to apologize to me ... your own convictions have always prompted you. You may not realize it, but this is a rare quality in a world where people don't like to take responsibility for their actions or to say, "I'm sorry."

Your sense of humor has brought me belly laughs and made me laugh so hard that I cry. You see laughter in situations and circumstances that bring joy to others. You are generous with your amazing smile, and you make others feel loved and accepted.

You look out for the underdog ... you stand up for those who do not have a voice in this world. God calls these things justice and mercy. In fact, in Micah 6:8, it tells us that what God requires of us is to act with justice and to love mercy and to walk humbly with Him. I see you doing these things as part of your character, not just when people are watching. You are genuine and never pretend to be someone who you're not.

You are smart. You have always learned quickly and have enjoyed learning. You may not see it now because learning is attached to school, but I know that you will be a lifelong learner in some way. You are fascinated with new information, new skills, and new places and people. Your winsome personality will open many doors for you and will give you many opportunities. Make sure that you recognize that God has given you these gifts and that it is not of yourself, and you will be used greatly for His kingdom.

I am confident that whatever you pursue, you will succeed. I believe in you!

Brendon, I love you with all my heart. You are someone who I would want to know even if you were not my son. I love the person that you are and the man that God is shaping you to be. As you end your years in middle school and begin your trek into high school and your adult years, please remember a few things:

1. You are loved unconditionally.

2. You are God's beloved child.

3. Commit your ways to God and you will succeed.

4. Trust in the Lord with all your heart and do not rely on your own understanding ... in all your ways acknowledge Him and He will make your paths straight!

5. Family is so important ... and so are family nights!

6. You were created for a special purpose ... discover it and live it!

You just will never know how proud you make me. Congratulations on finishing well, using your leadership, persevering even when you wanted to quit, for honoring your parents, being a good friend, being a wonderful and loving brother, and for just being YOU!

Love, Mom

A Father's Nod

Although words from a mother's heart to her son are an important aspect of his spiritual and emotional health, I have come to realize the importance of what I call "the father's nod." This is the moment when sons receive the "nod" from their dads that they have officially become men. Not just in a chronological sense, but in ways that run deeper than an age on a driver's license.

The nod says, "You are strong and confident. You have become what I had hoped you would become, and you have what it takes to make it in this world. I believe in you and am proud of who you are and who you are becoming. Well done, Son."

Boys look to their fathers for confirmation, and when they find it, they thrive. When they don't, they seek to find it the rest of their lives.

I remember a moment that took place between my husband and my son. There wasn't an exchange of words, to my knowledge, but it was powerful nonetheless. We were sailing as a family. My son was sixteen, and his girlfriend had come along with us that day. We ran into some heavy winds and high waves, and things became tense for a few moments. Both of our sails failed, and the wind was preventing us from untangling the mess.

Being the mom of two kids, my role has been to provide for and protect them alongside my husband. But in this pivotal moment, my husband didn't call upon me for assistance; he called upon our son. My husband told my son to go to the bow of the boat and physically unwind the sail from its tightly wrapped post. The wind was howling, and the waves were crashing on him, soaking him to the bone. I could see that the force of the wind and sail was requiring every ounce of his strength. With great effort and determination, my son was able to free the sail and allow my husband to put us back on track.

Later, I told this story to a male friend of mine. I mentioned how great my son must have felt in front of his girlfriend to have "saved the day." My friend corrected me and said, "Not in front of his girlfriend—in front of his *dad*." It was like a light bulb went on in my mind. Of course! My son felt like a man *in front of his dad* that day. And although I did not physically see it, my son received the "nod" from his father there on that boat in the middle of the ocean.

The Blessing Continues

And the nod continues to this day. Every idea, achievement, sacrifice, and conversation between my husband and son is marked by the words, "I love you, Son. I'm proud of you. Well done." What a beautiful gift of blessing my son receives from his father. I love my husband for this more than I can express.

This, however, is in sharp contrast to my husband's story. He never received the nod. It's not only painful, but it has proven to be one of his greatest struggles. His father died when Michael, my husband, was only twenty years old. Michael's British father had been distant, strict, and critical. Although my husband understood he was loved, only once in his life—when his father was on his deathbed—did Michael hear the words "I love you" from his dad.

When Michael decided to go into ministry full-time, his father showed disappointment, telling him it was a poor idea and that he would not be financially successful. In the twenty years that Michael knew his father, there were not many moments when his father helped him understand how to be a man, a father, or a husband. His father worked many hours and was rarely fully "present."

My husband confesses now that although he knew what he was doing, he couldn't stop looking for that nod in his professional and personal life. He worked hard to succeed in all aspects of life in order to somehow squelch the Criticizing parent voice of doubt that his father had implanted in his mind.

I recently asked him if someone else could have filled that role for him—the role of giving the nod. He paused and said that although more difficult, an uncle, a grandfather, a friend of his father's, or a spiritual mentor who chose to really "do life" with him could have given him the confidence to feel that he had received that very important affirmation.

For those fathers who are fathering today, I want to say something directly to you:

> *You cannot underestimate the importance of your part in giving your sons, and even your daughters, your affection and affirmation. Daughters, too, need to know that you see their beauty (inside and out), that they have your undivided attention when they talk to you, and that you love them no matter what. Above all things (your career, your interests, your financial portfolio), pay attention to how you are giving or not giving the nod. Whether you received it or not, you can pass on a new legacy of blessing to your children.*

Lauri's Story

So what if a father is not present in your children's lives? Let me tell you a story that may give you hope:

At forty, Lauri instantly became a widow and a single mom. Her greatest fear became reality when her husband of eighteen years, Doug, suddenly passed away. "My dreams were shattered, my future was very uncertain, and my only hope was Jesus," Lauri recalls. "Heaven became a very real place, and I longed for it."

That day was a blur. There were the phone calls inquiring about her husband's heart condition, arriving at the hospital and walking the cold halls of the ER, and having to tell her sons that their father was gone. But she never had to walk through those difficult, heart-wrenching experiences alone. "I quickly experienced how big my God was and is," Lauri says. "Had I not had my faith or my faith community, I don't think I would have healed."

At the time, Lauri's two sons were ten and twelve, the ages when boys seem to need a father the most. Who would usher them into adulthood and teach them what it meant to be Christian men in today's world? These young men, now in college, share how their faith community of men has come alongside their steps to manhood. Friends of their father, and other men in the church, made sure to include these two boys in father-son trips, celebrated their rites of passage, and took time to be at sporting events and other milestones. They have been prayed for and supported each step of the way.

This is the way God intended *His* family to respond to one another. God knew families would suffer loss and pain, and that no family would have the perfect life they anticipated. His provision was that we would, in His name, fill in the gaps for each other. No one family can provide for its needs in the powerful ways that the family of God can!

Before his death, Lauri's husband sacrificed much to serve others in the church. His sons were the recipients of the investment he had made. Others wanted to give back to his legacy of servanthood.

In the midst of raising our children in imperfect circumstances, we cannot afford to neglect serving and blessing others in our local churches. We build "family" in the truest sense of the word when we do so, and the dividends are eternal.

If you are a Criticizing parent, find redemption in allowing God to use your words for blessing instead of cursing. God can begin a legacy of "good speaking" from the ashes of where there has been none.

Reflect and Respond

1. Take some time to reflect on your family of origin. Did you receive words of blessing or words that tore you down? How have those words shaped you for good? How have they negatively shaped you or caused ongoing pain?

2. As you consider God's words of blessing upon your life in Christ, how do these perhaps shape or reshape your identity?

3. In what practical ways can you begin to discipline your words as a Criticizing parent and instead "scatter benedictions" to your children (and your spouse) on a regular basis?

4. Of the five biblical and practical steps that Trent and Smalley outline in *The Blessing*, which one do you desire to have God grow in you in the next few weeks and months?

5. As a father, how can you begin a path to give your children the "nod" regardless of whether it was given to you or not?

6. If the father of your children is not actively a part of their lives, in what ways can you allow your faith community to play a role in supporting and affirming your children? Pray that God will give you wisdom in this matter.

8

Living a Meaningful Family Mission

For the Absentee Parent

The best thing to spend on your child is your time.
Louise Hart

I recently received a beautiful piece of art from a friend. Its words were so compelling to me that I saw it as my to-do list for each day—even better, a divine *mission statement* for life. The words simply say:

> *Think Deeply*
> *Speak Gently*
> *Love Much*
> *Laugh a Lot*
> *Work Hard*

Give Freely
And Be Kind

A lot of people are talking about "being on mission" these days. We discuss what it means to live intentional lives full of purpose for God and others at every age. I'm amazed at how God is putting His plans on the hearts of *even small children*. And yet, many of us are off doing "the work of the Lord," or just working hard to get ahead, so that we not only neglect our missions, but we are absent from them.

The Absentee parent justifies her nonparticipation in her family life by saying that she is providing for them or making a better life for them. I have found that often these are just excuses to be away from the hard work of parenting and marriage, but I have also found that many people truly have good (but terribly misguided) motives.

Work and a paycheck, colleagues and business plans, traveling and intellectual stimulation all feel incredibly satisfying because these things are part of a greater mission. The mission is often the increase of a company's bank account, or a service industry to help people, or providing basic care for people's daily lives. At the end of a day or a quarter or a fiscal year, an Absentee parent can look back and see her progress toward that mission.

But what about progress in family life? These things feel less meaningful—or so it seems. There are bills to pay, sure, but the bottom line rarely feels increased. There are no paychecks in parenting, parents are overworked and unappreciated, and there is rarely if ever true intellectual stimulation.

But for the Absentee parent who is "married" to work (or pleasure), *there is* a far greater and compelling mission at hand. And our children are ready and willing to succeed in this mission with us.

Ruby's Story

I know of a little girl named Ruby, who at a young age decided to do something that would have a lasting impact. Her mom supported her and made her dream a reality. This is her story:

Ruby lives in Georgetown, Texas, a small community outside of Austin. When she was just five years old, Ruby overheard a conversation about Free Wheelchair Mission, a nonprofit organization that provides wheelchairs to the disabled poor in developing nations. When Ruby heard that more than one hundred million people in these countries can't walk and must crawl on the ground or be carried by loved ones, she decided she needed to do something.

So Ruby took it upon herself to begin collecting coins she found around the house. When her mother noticed and asked why she was collecting money, Ruby answered, "I'm saving to buy a wheelchair for someone who can't afford one." Ruby's mom agreed this was a worthy cause, so she set up a chore-and-reward system for Ruby to earn the $63.94 needed to buy one wheelchair. It worked so well they decided to share the news at Ruby's school. The excitement began to grow, and Ruby's prekindergarten class took on the challenge, using their spring break to raise money for wheelchairs.

Ruby's mom spurred on the other parents to give their children ownership of the project, encouraging them to be creative about how to raise the money to give others the gift of mobility. One of the boys in the class organized a lemonade stand and called it "Lemonade for Love."

At the end of two weeks, this class of four- and five-year-olds earned enough money to purchase four wheelchairs! Four lives around the world would be transformed because of one preschooler's compassionate heart. And that compassion spread into the community, inspiring others to give.

I think what inspires me most about Ruby's story is how her mom took the tender seed of Ruby's heart to help mobilize it into something tangible. She wasn't absent physically, spiritually, or emotionally. She was attentive to see a seed in her daughter and made the sacrifices necessary to water it into fruition. As we endeavor to become spiritually healthy families, each one of us will play a vital part in allowing our homes to be on mission in the middle of our everyday lives.

And we can't accomplish this when we are not present.

Writing a Family Mission Statement

Organizations and institutions of all types and sizes create mission statements. A mission statement becomes a "north star," so to speak, reminding the owners who they are and where they want their companies or organizations to go. The truly bold are those owners who post their companies' missions on their beverage cups, their walls, and in their print media. They make it clear who they are in such a way that you, the consumer, can measure their success.

For example, the mission statement of a popular burger restaurant, In-N-Out, says In-N-Out exists to:

> Give customers the freshest, highest quality foods
> you can buy and provide them with friendly service
> in a sparkling clean environment.[1]

When I eat a burger at this establishment, I can assess if the company is meeting its mission. I can determine if my food is fresh, if I sense my importance by the employees' actions, and if the environment is clean.

Getting to the Heart (and Soul) of the Matter

What if our families were so bold? What if we got to the heart and soul of why our families exist and why they are made up of such unique individuals? What if Absentee parents simply began to show up and work hard to accomplish new goals and new plans that would produce a different type of dividend? What if this parent stopped trying to just "check out" or "move up" and said: "We are here in this household together. And as broken and bizarre as we sometimes are—why are we here in this family? What are we uniquely poised to accomplish in our years here together? Whether there are just two of us in our home or ten of us, what have we been divinely commissioned to do in this world?"

The answer to this makes a compelling mission statement.

A Family Mission Statement

When my children were late elementary and early middle school-aged, my husband and I decided we needed such a statement. We wanted to create a trajectory for our family's values and hopes—something by which we (and others) could judge our efforts. It felt risky, but we jumped in.

So there we sat, looking at our children, asking them to describe the type of family they hoped to live in. At first, it was simply a "deer in the headlights" moment. I could hear their thoughts, *Can't we just play video games or watch TV?* But my husband began to elaborate about why this would be important. He told our kids to get into the car because we were going out to eat. Thinking that they were getting out of our "home-work" assignment, they eagerly complied.

Within a few minutes we were at a local restaurant—one of their favorites. On the wall was a mission statement. My husband asked our son to read it out loud, and he did. Then he asked both of our kids if the restaurant had lived up to those words and why. We had a good conversation over pasta and bread sticks, then returned home. Then we readdressed the subject of our family mission statement. This time, the conversation had more passion.

We asked, "What kind of family do you want to be known for?" Our kids' words blurted out so fast that I had to grab a piece of paper to write them all down: *grace-giving, loving, generous, honest, Christ-centered, forgiving, compassionate,* and *a place of refuge.* Refuge? Really? That was from my eleven-year-old son. I didn't think that was a word he even understood. My husband added *attention to God's Word* and *obedient.* I added *joyful.*

Now the Hard Part

Then came the hard part: trying to write all these words into a concise sentence. Effective mission statements are said to be easily memorized—something you could put on a T-shirt or coffee mug. We wanted to honor everyone's words and thoughts, but we wanted it to be memorable, something that would easily come to mind.

As I played with our words, using connecting words to bring clarity, this was what we penned together as a family that night:

> *We, the Anthony Family, choose to live by faith in Jesus Christ in a grace-giving environment characterized by: providing refuge and compassion to those in need and demonstrating love and joy in all circumstances through the daily obedience to God's Word.*

We tried not to overthink it. We knew that it couldn't perfectly capture everything, but we trusted that God would use our feeble attempt to put His mission for us into words. I had it printed and framed and put in a prominent place in our house. I wanted us to see it every day. I wanted our family members, and others who came into our home, to be able to assess our effectiveness in comparison to our hopes and dreams. It felt gutsy—even arrogant at times—but we knew that it was important enough to try, even if we failed.

And fail we did. I can't tell you the number of times when I was grumbling about a trial and saw the words "demonstrating … joy in all circumstances"—ugh! Or when one of us withheld forgiveness and read "choose to live … in a grace-giving environment." We also had others who lived with us over the years (because we wanted to provide "refuge ... to those in need"), and we knew they were able to see our sinfulness on any given day too.

But what is the alternative? Make no statement of hope? Make no declaration of mission? Continue to be absent? That's the easy way out! No one will judge you, and you need not judge yourself either, right?

Choosing Courage

Families who are becoming spiritually healthy choose to be courageous. *Being absent is the coward's way out.* It takes courage to be in it day in and day out and to stay connected to the vitality of intimacy with your spouse and children.

And, just when you think you are not measuring up, perhaps you will be surprised. Perhaps God will give you a dose of grace to encourage you. This happened to my family. At a reception for an award for my husband, a gentleman who lived with us for five months got up to speak. He shared that he saw our mission statement when he first arrived at our home and thought, "How sweet." Translation: "These are nice words, but I doubt they are anything more than that."

However, he went on to express the many ways that he, in fact, saw our family members successfully living out these words. I cried as I listened to him, recognizing that by God's grace, He had not only shaped who and what we wanted to be, but had also accomplished many of these very things in our lives.

Our family mission impacted the decisions we made. It was the grid for our priorities. It kept us engaged when we wanted to check out.

Because of this statement, we decided to turn our garage into a youth lounge where *anyone* could come at *any time*. We left the doors open, put in a TV and a sofa, stocked a small fridge with food and drinks, and welcomed our community into our lives. And boy did they come! We used our guest room for individuals to stay for a season while they were in transition. These ended up being mature Christian models for our children to live among and to be influenced by.

These types of decisions must be made swiftly and with intentionality. The opportune times we have been given will evaporate without us even noticing. Ask yourself right now, "How will I intentionally and strategically create and live out the priorities of our family's mission?"

Let's Get Started!

Of course, a family mission needs to be given life—words! Take some time to think through your family in all its unique contributions. If your children are old enough, let them be a part of the mission's creation. I know children as young as five who have contributed to this in powerful ways. If you have infants and toddlers, you can still do this on your own as a couple or as a single parent with the assistance of someone who is coparenting with you or an engaged family member.

In the upcoming pages, you will find some questions to work through together. Remember, this is not a race. You may find that you need to camp out on one or more of these questions for a while in order to really extract what is at the core of your heart in that area. Take your time, but don't overthink it.

Also, I cannot stress enough spending time in prayer to make sure that your hopes and goals are God's hopes and goals for your family. This exercise alone allows you to remember that you are each here to glorify Him with your time, gifts, and resources. Pray to have the mind of Christ as you seek His plan for the breath He has given each of you.

Perhaps this prayer will help guide your hearts and minds as you begin:

> *Dear heavenly Father,*
>
> *We acknowledge that You are Lord over all things—including each of us in this family and the lives that You have given us. We do not desire to be individuals who cohabitate together under one roof, run away from our responsibilities, or busy ourselves so much that we are not present. But rather, we desire to be a family woven together to accomplish Your plans for us. Guide us with Your wisdom and with Your words in order that we might discover together the joy of serving You each day with all that You have entrusted to us. We trust You to continue to make us into the kind of family that puts You on display to others in all circumstances. Thank You in advance for what You are going to do in and through us.*

So What Are You Waiting For?

Proverbs 14:22 states, "But those who plan what is good find love and faithfulness." In the planning of our desires for our family, we honor God and tell Him we want to live our days on this earth wisely. We know that our lives are like vapors and that we are only here for a short time. Therefore, the intentionality of living with a purpose gives great meaning for generations to come—even after we are gone.

Our lives can have a generational impact. Think about it—in what ways did your parents, grandparents, and even great grandparents impact your life for good? For bad? Either way, we make an imprint—not just on our children's lives, but for generations to come. So in the midst of carpool schedules, grocery shopping, job duties, and the bills that need to be paid … STOP. Stop now, and make time to write your family's mission.

Show up.

Be present.

If you put it off until you "have time," you never will.

Questions to Consider in Writing a Mission Statement

(These are also listed in appendix B of this book, which you can copy as a handout for your family members.)

- What kind of family life do you want your children to remember?
- What kind of atmosphere do you want to have in your home?
- What kind of family do you want to be known for?

- What kind of parent do you want to be?
- What behaviors do you want your family members to demonstrate?
- What goals will you have for your children at various stages of their lives?
- What are some of your fondest childhood memories?
- What painful experiences did you have in your family that you do not feel would benefit your children if replicated?
- What kinds of biblical qualities do you believe children should exhibit?
- What mode of discipline do you feel is best in your home?
- What changes do you need to make in order to allow your family to have more time/fun together?
- What perspectives should your children encounter other than the ones that they are naturally exposed to? (Think of culture, economics, politics, and so on.)
- What are you willing to sacrifice in order to accomplish these plans?

Reflect and Respond

(These questions are also listed in appendix C of this book, which you can copy as a handout for your family members.)

1. As you begin to think through your mission statement, write down three things that you want for your family and children as an *end result*. What do you hope to see when they are young adults someday? (For example, to live lives in accordance with God's laws and grace, to reflect the character of God, to demonstrate a life of love, and so on.) These are essentially value statements.

   Write them here:

   _____

   _____

   _____

   _____

   _____

   _____

2. Think about these desires and visions for your family that you just wrote down. In what ways could you be a part of that end result? Think of three words that give you a place in that. Words such as: *model, nurture, encourage and hold accountable, demonstrate, come alongside of, inspire*, and so on.

   _____

   _____

   _____

   _____

   _____

   _____

Attach these words to the prior vision words (in question 1) and then begin to add *linking words* (such as *through, and, with, for*). Write a rough draft and don't overthink it—you can always revise later.

Pray about your participation in your child's spiritual growth and write your thoughts on question 2 here:

_____

_____

_____

_____

_____

_____

3. Using your answers from questions 1 and 2, begin to write your family mission statement here:

_____

_____

_____

_____

_____

_____

_____

An Example

One set of parents answered question 1 with these desires:

- Living according to God's laws
- Reflecting God's character in caring for the poor
- Living lives of love

They went on to answer question 2 with these words that allowed them to be a part of this process:

- Model
- Come alongside
- Nurture

As they blended these thoughts together, this was their mission statement:

> *We, the Jensen family, will endeavor, with God's help, to model lives that are living in accordance to God's laws and grace, to come alongside our children to help those who are poor, both in life and spirit, and to nurture each child to reflect the character of God by choosing to demonstrate a life of love to everyone we come in contact with.*

When you finish your family mission statement, it will be unique to you and your family members. No one will accomplish those hopes and dreams quite like your family can and will. I encourage you to print and frame this statement and put it in a place of prominence in your home. Perhaps a smaller version of it would be appropriate to put in each of your bedrooms.

Remind your family members often that this is not just a one-time exercise or a poetic piece of art, but "marching orders" for what you sense God desires of your family at this time in history! What could be more compelling than this in a world concerned with mission, to give you, your children, your family, a divine purpose?

9

Beyond Good Behavior and Chore Charts

For the Spiritually Healthy Family

I looked back … and realized I had spent 10 years trying to convince kids to behave Christianly without actually teaching them Christianity. And that was a pretty serious conviction. You can say, "Hey kids, be more forgiving because the Bible says so," or "Hey kids, be more kind because the Bible says so!" But that isn't Christianity, it's morality…. We're drinking a cocktail that's a mix of the Protestant work ethic, the American dream, and the gospel. And we've intertwined them so completely that we can't tell them apart anymore. Our gospel has become a gospel of following your dreams and being good so God will make all your dreams come true. It's the Oprah god.

Phil Vischer, in an interview with *World Magazine*

Feed the dog. Wash the dishes. Make your bed. Take out the trash. Do these sound familiar? These, among others, make up the decades-tested and child-protested "chore chart." You know, the one that is prominently placed in your home on the refrigerator or in the laundry room? Each family member's name is listed next to a set of things that need to be done around the house. Chore charts give instruction, accountability, and some sort of reward or penalty system. They are used to motivate children (and let's face it, even spouses) toward responsibility.

I also know families whose chore charts are used for more than household duties. Some have used this model for encouraging or disciplining behavior. These charts include things such as good attitude, getting along with siblings, showing respect for Mom and Dad, and first-time obedience. In such an instance, children have visual feedback about their behavior on a regular basis. No star in one column might serve to motivate a small child to do better the following day.

Good Morals

Chore charts are effective to a point, especially if our goal is to get through the day or week with a tidier home and better-behaved children. But what if there was something more inspiring for our families on our spiritual journeys together? What if God has something more in store for us than chore charts and good behavior?

Much of how we approach spiritual formation in our homes and in our churches comes from an educational model. In school, our teachers tell us what we need to do or learn and then they hold us accountable through tests, charts, and reward/discipline systems. We are evaluated against a "norm" that measures our progress against others in our classes, our grades, even our nations.

We can begin to think that our role as parents is to create a home where we cultivate moral training, good behavior, or "how to look like a Christian in ten easy steps." This has been tempting for me as a parent, because good behavior looks so much like faith on *the outside*. The children look well mannered, they go to church, they bring their Bibles, they memorize their verses, they say they're sorry when they've hurt someone, they go on missions trips, they give a portion of their money as an offering, and they participate in selfless acts of kindness. When we've taught them those things, it's tempting for us to say to ourselves, "Good job! Look how *spiritual* my child is!"

In his article "How to Raise a Pagan Kid in a Christian Home," Barrett Johnson said:

> The gospel is not about making bad people moral, but about making dead people alive. If we teach morality without the transforming power of the gospel and the necessity of a life fully surrendered to God's will, then we are raising moral pagans....
>
> Do you teach your kids "be good because the Bible tells you to" or do you teach your kids that they will never be good without Christ's offer of grace? There is a huge difference. One leads to moralism; the other leads to brokenness. One leads to self-righteousness; the other leads to a life that

realizes that Christ is everything and that nothing
else matters.[1]

Certainly when children are young, moral behavior is indeed
what we teach them. We tell our children, "Say 'thank you'"; "Don't
hit your brother"; "Tell the truth." We don't debate with them about
this; these are the rules. "Just do it because I say so!" In the moments
of teaching these things, we almost don't even care about our children's hearts, because these are simply things people do to live in this
world in proximity to other people.

But as our children grow up, parents often don't grow with
them. A father may have a fifteen-year-old son, but he is still saying,
"Don't do drugs"; "Don't have sex with your girlfriend"; "Say you're
sorry"; "Be nice to your sister." When we do this, we continue to use
moral behavior tactics at the stage when moral development needs to
be transcended by spiritual development.

In spiritual development, the child's *heart* matters—not just his
or her actions. This is the stage at which we need to let the Holy
Spirit come in and act in that child's life. Yet if we don't make that
transition, we fall into the temptation of making our homes about
just being a really *good person*. But really good people are not what
Jesus asked for. He asked for people of faith. And faith is so much
messier (and harder to measure) than moral behavior.

Envision a Future

Chapter 2 included a snapshot of what a spiritually healthy family
could possibly look like with God's help and a commitment of faith:

In contrast to the six dysfunctional parenting styles stands the offer of hope from God to live in relationship with Him, pursuing His kingdom while living on His script. While far from perfect, the Spiritually Healthy parent is a parent who walks each day, step by step, with God as his guide.

Becoming a spiritually healthy family means you will allow God to call the shots for you and your family members and that you look to Him to give you wisdom instead of relying on your own strength and "great ideas". Because you realize you are a work in progress yourself, you offer your children grace when needed, while helping them see the corrected path that God desires all His children to follow.

You recite the following things each day, because, deep down you know them to be true:

- "I recognize that my child has been entrusted to me by God and that I need His guidance to raise her."
- "I know I live in a sinful world, but I will seek to put God's character on display in my home in everyday situations."
- "I know there is higher calling as a parent than controlling my child's behavior—and that is forming his faith."
- "I seek to grow spiritually myself, knowing that the overflow of this will have a positive impact on my child."

Children raised by the Spiritually Healthy parent often grow up knowing God, loving others, living a life of meaning, and recognizing that this world is not their ultimate home.

After reading the other six options, I hope your heart is confident that God's Directorship in your life and in the lives of your family members is the only way to fulfill the abundant life Jesus promised. In order to receive this abundance, however, you must choose to live on His script each day—as written. This will take faith.

Christian Education

Let's contrast this type of faith life adventure with the common model of faith found in a purist's approach to Christian education. Children, during their time spent at church, are often taught about faith by memorizing books of the Bible and the characters and events within its stories.

As students, we learn the Ten Commandments and the Fruit of the Spirit as lists, which guide us how to behave and/or not behave. These efforts, much like the school system, work well when our children are young and their thinking is concrete. However, when our children get older, they begin to question. They are influenced by their culture and peers, and the often simplistic Sunday school answers that once appeased them no longer satisfy.

If we don't help our children graduate from a basic moral formation to a more vibrant spiritual formation, we run the risk that they will miss out on *lifetime faith*. And at the end of our allotted time as parents to raise our kids, we want our children to possess authentic, enduring relationships with Jesus.

We don't want to say, "Well, we raised Ryder in the church and taught him good morals and values in our home. We don't know why his childhood faith didn't last now that he's in college." You see, that's the problem—when we simply feel satisfied with our efforts to nurture a "childhood faith," it may become just that.

Something More Than Good Morals

Christian educator and philosopher John Coe teaches that the Christian life is about a certain kind of obedience and effort, but not the kind of obedience that we usually think about in our striving to be "Christian." Rather, it's the opening up of the heart to a relationship. It's a dependence upon the indwelling Spirit. Abiding in Christ. *This* is our obedience. This is what the spiritual life is actually all about.

Coe once stated in a lecture, "I don't want to be a *good boy* anymore. I don't want to try to fix myself. I can't fix myself. I want to learn to give up on the project and open more deeply to Christ's work and the work of the Spirit in my deep. But I am still daily tempted by moral formation."[2]

Think of how ironic this is. Who on earth would be *tempted* to be moral? We commonly think of ourselves as tempted to be immoral, but the life of the Christian includes both. We in fact do find ourselves in the temptation of moral formation and therefore we pass this on to our children. We have this little "guilt meter" inside us, put there by our loving parents, the church, and our sinful human natures. It beckons us to want to make ourselves *better*.

The apostle Paul knew that we would be tempted by this very thing. He wrote this to the early Galatian church:

> O foolish Galatians! Who has bewitched you? It
> was before your eyes that Jesus Christ was publicly

portrayed as crucified. Let me ask you only this: Did you receive the Spirit by works of the law or by hearing with faith? Are you so foolish? Having begun by the Spirit, are you now being perfected by the flesh? (Gal. 3:1–3 ESV)

We have the opportunity to allow our children to think differently—to think "Yes, I'm sinful, yes, I'm broken, but I can't fix myself. Only the Holy Spirit can." This will require our children to have intimate relationships with Him, to know Him, to hear His voice, to depend upon Him, and not to get up tomorrow to simply *try harder*.

Paul wrote in Galatians 4:19, that it was as if he were longing "in the pains of childbirth until Christ is formed in you." It's that simple. When we eliminate all the other distractions in child-rearing, we ultimately want to see Jesus in our children. We don't need high and lofty explanations of spiritual formation that only the really smart or really spiritual people will understand. Instead, we need to be able to wake up every day in our lives and those of our family members and say, "*How is Christ being formed in me … in you?*" It's not just about a chart that can tell us if we're doing better; it's about a relationship with a perfect Savior who is making us, His disciples, more like Himself each day.

What Is a Disciple?

Being a true disciple of Christ means that I am walking in the steps that He walks. I make the volitional choice to die to myself each day and let Him "direct the play" as He sees it. The process of discipleship is far more about "following" than "obtaining perfection." Yet I wonder if, by my words and actions, I have communicated to my children that discipleship is about being perfect—or at least looking perfect.

In her book *Strengthening the Soul of Your Leadership*, Ruth Haley Barton described discipleship as a

> process that goes far beyond mere behavioral tweaks to work deep, fundamental changes at the very core of our being. In the process of transformation the Spirit of God moves us from behaviors motivated by fear and self-protection to trust and abandonment to God; from selfishness and self-absorption to freely offering the gifts of the authentic self; from the ego's desperate attempts to control the outcomes of our lives to an ability to give ourselves over to the will of God which is often the foolishness of this world.[3]

Barton warns us to not think of such issues of change as glorified self-help strategies. Change really is something God must do in us since it goes to the dark places in our souls—places even we are unaware of. The surface stuff is easy. It's the deep stuff that we need professional help for. And the only professional qualified to take our sin and make us pure *is Jesus*!

Sometimes I find myself thinking that this process is something that is my responsibility alone. In his book *Invitation to a Journey: A*

Road Map for Spiritual Formation, Robert Mulholland illustrates this when he said:

> Discipleship is perceived as "my" spiritual life and tends to be defined by actions that ensure its possession. Thus the endless quest for techniques, methods, programs by which we hope to achieve spiritual fulfillment. The hidden premise behind all of this is the unquestioned assumptions that we alone are in control of our spirituality … [and] of our relationship with God.[4]

The Ten Environments

It's imperative that we teach and model true discipleship for our children. We want them to understand that this is a formative work *God* is doing through His Spirit, and that by following Him and submitting to Him, we have the opportunity to partner with Him in it. We must commit ourselves to spending time in God's Word, to investing time and service in a growing community of other Christians, and to making prayer a regular part of everyday events, not just in crisis times. But by no means can we ever achieve perfection, godliness, or goodness in our efforts—no matter how noble our intentions are.

One of the best ways that I have found to practically put this into practice is through the "ten environments" that I outline in my book *Spiritual Parenting*. These environments help me understand *my part* in the spiritual health of my family. God does the hard work of supernatural transformation, and my part is to be faithful to create an intentional environment in my home where I am not getting in the way of what God is doing. Rather, I am putting God on display in everyday situations. (See appendix A for a list of the ten environments.)

If we don't understand this (as well as help our children understand), we will fall back on the educational model of spirituality and faith. This model by itself seldom has abundant life or lifelong faith attached to its efforts.

A New Wineskin

In many ways, the paradigm shift from "achieving proper behavior" to "a life posture of faith formation from the inside out" could be compared to Jesus's words about embracing a new wineskin:

> Neither do people pour new wine into old wineskins. If they do, the skins will burst, the wine will run out and the wineskins will be ruined. No, they pour new wine into new wineskins, and both are preserved. (Matt. 9:17)

His original audience would have understood an old wineskin as one that had already expanded during the fermentation process from grape juice to wine. This expansion would have taken place when the bladder being used was still fresh and pliable. Once expanded, it dried out. To put new wine into an old wineskin would cause it to crack or burst open. Those listening to Jesus would have known that you put new wine in new wineskins.

Jesus used this image to compare the religious system prevalent in His society at that time with the "new wine" He was about to pour out. The new wine was an opportunity for people to no longer have to earn a relationship with God through observance of the Law but rather to experience God in a relationship through the power of His Spirit, who was poured out after Christ's death satisfied the price of sin.

This paradigm shift in thinking and acting required a new understanding. The old ways of doing things would no longer be useful for what was to come. In fact, those not interested in the new wineskin would lose out on both the new covenant and the relationship with God.

The Poster Child of Good Religion

If anyone is the poster child for this change of thinking, it would be the apostle Paul. Before he was authoring books of the Bible and spreading the gospel on missionary journeys, he was killing Christians. And not because he was a bad guy either—quite the opposite. Known as Saul at the time, he was the best of the best. A Pharisee (a Jewish religious leader) among Pharisees. Taught by the best rabbis and an impeccable student and follower of the Law.

He believed that Jesus and His followers were threatening the purity of their faith in God. He knew all the right stuff and had all the right behaviors, but he didn't truly *know* God.

One day, while on a journey, Saul had a real-life encounter with God. It's recorded in Acts 9. A bright light blinded him, and a voice questioned him: "Saul, Saul, why do you persecute me?" When Saul asked who was speaking, the voice replied, "I am Jesus, whom you are persecuting." Wow! That must have been an incredible moment of realization.

What strikes me about Paul's life was how he could have "missed it." If he could miss it with all that he knew and did, then certainly we and our children are at risk of missing it too if we get focused on the wrong stuff.

It really comes down to how we will ultimately define successful faith. Is it merely good morals and good behavior? Paul, toward the end of his life, defined success as this:

> However, I consider my life worth nothing to me; my only aim is to finish the race and complete the task the Lord Jesus has given me—the task of testifying to the good news of God's grace. (Acts 20:24)

So what is the task that the Lord Jesus has given to each member of your family? As you discover and accomplish this each day, you are living out a meaningful and successful faith.

Determining that task will require *a relationship* with Jesus, and a relationship with Him comes from experiencing Him, not just knowing about Him. Throughout history, we have often set aside *relationships* for *religion,* and in doing so, lost why we were following Jesus in the first place. Let's take a quick historical look at why we have been made to believe that good parents hand down a "religious system" to their children.

From Risen Savior to Religious Systems

The Christian movement officially began on the day of Pentecost when God poured out His Spirit on the people who believed in Jesus, the risen Savior. The early church was led by God's Spirit and functioned as a living and breathing example of God's work within His followers to transform their lives and their families. However, as the church grew and spread like a wildfire, the leaders began to initiate structures to systematize their efforts to the masses.

The systematization of the Church led to:

- Format
- Curriculum
- Structure
- Councils and boards
- Leadership hierarchy
- Doctrine and tradition

In some ways these things were helpful to educate the vast numbers of new Christ followers, but in some ways the systems robbed the church of the intimacy of being in relationship with God through Jesus Christ. The church floundered during the Middle Ages, the centuries when the church and world floundered in intentional spiritual growth and manifestations.

An Era of Enlightenment

In the fifteenth century, the Renaissance began in Italy and soon spread throughout Europe. The Reformation of the sixteenth century was in many ways sparked by the Renaissance. Later the influence of the Renaissance formed how southern Europe defined Christianity while the Reformation greatly impacted northern Europe.

The Renaissance, or "rebirth," was known for its emphasis on art, literature, music, expression and emotion, and philosophy. The Reformation, or "reform," was known for the Ninety-five Theses (which Martin Luther nailed on the door of Castle Church in Wittenberg, Germany), biblical accuracy, independent learning, intellectualism and understanding, and literacy. Both of these movements were important to our Christian history in that God's people were awakened to truth in both intellectual and emotional forms.

Sunday School

A few hundred years later, in 1780, Sunday school was started by Robert Raikes of England. His desire was to see working-class children receive education even though they were in the workforce Monday through Friday (and sometimes Saturdays too). Raikes held "school" on Sunday and found that the Bible was the best textbook for all sorts of learning. This Sunday school movement spread like wildfire throughout Europe, and soon adults and children alike were learning the Bible from a scholastic model.

The United States was founded by immigrants and their descendants from England and other northern European nations.

They kept this structure of Sunday school for Bible teaching even after children were no longer working during the week. The early American churches kept this time for biblical instruction in addition to a Sunday worship service. To this day, you will find many churches that offer a Sunday school program during one hour and a worship service during a second hour.

Sunday school is often based on a Christian education model that teaches spiritual matters much like one would teach science, math, or history. There is also a model that was influenced by things seen during the Renaissance. The chart below shows a comparison of how the two models might best be understood:

Christian Education	*Spiritual Formation*
• Intellectual	• Experiential
• Dogmatic and didactic	• Subjective and intuitive
• Memorization	• Meditation
• Exegetical Study	• Sacred Study
• Corporate	• Personal
• Recitation	• Reflection
• Rubric Assessment	• Personal Assessment
• Application	• Response
• Extrinsic Motivation	• Intrinsic Motivation

While Christian education and spiritual formation are not things that are at odds with each other, they do have some distinctions. I believe that much of what we are passing on in our homes is commonly a model from the educational side of things.

When we can bring some of what spiritual formation has to offer, I believe we give our children a full view of their lives in Christ: both knowledge and personal experiences.

Bible Study versus Sacred Study

Let me illustrate a difference between the two approaches. I once met a young man who had not grown up in the church. He looked at my Bible with dismay. He saw that it was well-worn (even torn), and that I had marked it with every pen color and highlighter imaginable. To me, my Bible is a study tool. I love my Bible. I want to learn from it and understand it. I have marked up this one Bible since I was in high school. It has seen many miles with me. When I open it, I am familiar. I shuffle pages effortlessly, knowing exactly where I am going and why.

His approach was different. While I was raised with an emphasis more on Christian education, my friend had been exposed to more of a spiritual formation model. He picked up his Bible before me with reverence. Before even opening it, he bowed to silently pray. As he turned each page, I noticed that each was pristine without markings. He spoke softly when he read a favorite verse. He saw the reading of his Bible as a holy encounter.

Neither approach is wrong. Both are good, in fact. But I was challenged that day by my new friend because he gave me a glimpse into something I had never considered before. That is the beauty of the intersection between Christian education and spiritual formation.

Understanding Other Categories

Let's briefly unpack the other categories in the chart as well.

Intellectual versus Experiential

This describes where the main focus is. In the intellectual category, educators are concerned with what is known and learned. In the experiential category, educators are looking to what is perceived and felt.

Dogmatic versus Subjective

This describes how we look at certain aspects of our faith. In the dogmatic camp, an educator is placing value on everyone agreeing to certain things in order to ensure that truth remains pure. This is often how doctrine was written and why we find so many different denominations within the Christian church—these groups of people were dogmatic in their interpretation of Scripture. Conversely, the subjective camp doesn't water down the foundational truths of our faith, but they leave room for questions and not knowing all the answers. They embrace the mystery of God and don't need to have answers to everything.

Memorization versus Meditation

This describes a certain focus on God's Word, and both are biblical. The Bible commands us to "hide God's Word in our hearts" but also equally gives importance to meditating on Scripture "both day and night." To memorize means we can recall the words, and to meditate means that we are reviewing what those words mean in a way that produces a different thought or action.

Corporate versus Personal

This describes how spiritual growth best takes place. In the corporate camp, we would say that going to church and being in small groups are the best way to grow, while those in the personal camp feel that personal prayer, reflection, and Bible study—where we are most honest before God—yields the most growth.

Recitation versus Reflection

This describes what we do once we have studied or memorized God's Word. We can either recite it back to someone to show that we have learned it, or we can reflect on what it is saying and compare that to our own lives.

Rubric Assessment versus Personal Assessment

This describes how we measure a person's spiritual growth. One assessment has a rubric or standard of where a person should be at a certain age or after a certain number of years as a Christian, while the other is more adaptive to the individual. It sheds light on a person's willingness and ability to grow rather than on a certain point on a growth chart.

Application versus Response

This describes what is done after hearing God's Word. Some teachers place emphasis on how they instruct us to apply what is learned or how we change our actions accordingly. Others, however, believe we should simply respond to God through confession, thanksgiving, or worship, and He will instruct us on what to do next.

Extrinsic Motivation versus Intrinsic Motivation

This describes how we are motivated to learn, change, or adopt new approaches to faith formation. In the extrinsic camp, we are rewarded or disciplined for either adhering or failing to adhere to new information, while in the intrinsic camp educators hope to inspire us to grow or change based on our inner convictions or love relationships with God, regardless of compensation or judgment.

Some have compared the two philosophies of spiritual education in these terms:

Christian Education

External listening—gaining knowledge through books, teachers, and resources

Obedience—changing behavior

Trying harder—striving to work harder after disobedience occurs

Spiritual Formation

Internal listening—learning to discern God's voice

Desiring to obey—wanting to follow God's voice

Obeying in the power of the Holy Spirit—recognizing that it's more about learning to abide in Christ

Both/And

I wonder if the "more" that Jesus has in mind for us and our children, the more than good behavior and chore charts, is really this awakening to the both/and. What if this abundant life of being His is found in a blend of Christian education and spiritual formation, *together*? Each has a rich history for us to glean from. Each has biblical support. Each has something that this world will demand from us. Each offers us a piece of our lives in Christ.

It's easy to just do what we know, what we are familiar with. But raising kids in spiritually healthy homes is not easy. It is worth it, however!

If this chapter has you wondering how you can bring some of the richness of spiritual formation to the solid foundation of Christian education in your home, then allow me to introduce you to a great monthly family resource I am a part of producing called *HomeFront: A Spiritual Parenting Resource*. This monthly resource will empower you to bring to life the ten environments described in my book *Spiritual Parenting* in fun and innovative ways. You can subscribe to this free digital resource at HomeFrontMag.com, or you can purchase a physical subscription to be sent to your home as well.

In addition, creating faith milestones and celebrating rites of passage are also effective ways to "mark your journey" in becoming a spiritually healthy family. The next chapter will offer suggestions and thoughtful perspectives on the role of "remembering and celebrating" how far God has brought us.

Reflect and Respond

1. Take some time to reflect on how you were raised. Were you raised in the church? If so, was it more a Christian educational model or a spiritual formation model? How was that expressed?

2. What did you glean from your experience in the church? If you were not raised in the church, what influences shaped your current spirituality?

3. What was damaging from your experience in the church? If you were not raised in the church, what influences in the world damaged your perception of God?

4. How do you view the abundant life in relationship to living a spiritually healthy faith?

5. What things would you like your children to experience that you did in your early faith formation? What things would you like to do differently in your home?

6. If you are married, are you and your spouse in agreement on these things? How can you learn and grow together so that your children will have a well-rounded faith experience beyond good behavior and morals?

Remember and Celebrate the Abundant Life

Rites of Passage for Our Children

In times past there were rituals of passage that conducted
a boy into manhood, where other men passed along the
wisdom and responsibilities that needed to be shared.
But today we have no rituals. We are not conducted
into manhood; we simply find ourselves there.

Kent Nerburn, *Letters to My Son*

Peter Pan and the Lost Boys made their home in Neverland, a place where no one ever had to grow up. In many ways, it seems that Christianity's children have somehow fallen into a spiritual Neverland of sorts, where parents and the church are struggling to pass on mature faith from one generation to the next. In recent decades, however, parents have been made re-aware of their responsibility to help their children transition from childhood to adulthood, not just physically but spiritually as well.

This concept assumes there are certain *rites of passage* children must go through in order to reach maturity. However, smack-dab in the middle of childhood and adulthood are the dreaded teen years.

Confusion about how to communicate with this age group has haunted parents for many years. Mark Twain gave an amusing piece of advice concerning adolescence when he declared his preferred method of interacting with teenagers: "When a boy turns thirteen, put him in a barrel and feed him through the knothole. When he turns sixteen, plug up the hole." This humorous advice reflects parental frustration about what to do with adolescents who are struggling to transition from childhood to adulthood.

Take for example this exchange between a teenage daughter and her father, via text messaging. The daughter had been grounded and was trying to get her father to change his mind about letting her go out for the evening. What's worse than the "wearing us down" methodology so many teens use? *Spiritual* manipulation.

> **Daughter:** Is there any way to convince you to let me *go hear about God* tonight?

> **Dad:** Probably not, honey. But you are welcome to read the Bible or download a sermon or something like that if you want to learn about God from the comfort of your own home. Sorry.

Daughter: But you're *making* me move. I only have a few opportunities of growing closer in my *relationship with God* with my friends and with *my beloved small group leader.*

[pause]

And I already missed so much this week ... that's enough punishment!

[pause]

Plus I never even get to *go to church* because of *serving* in Children's Ministry.

[pause]

LOVE ME!

Dad: Sorry. No can do. And you know I love you so I'm not going to fall for that one.

Daughter: Daddy, come on! *Your daughter loves Jesus.* That's more than most dads can say ...

Dad: That is true. Go Jesus!!! But the answer is still no.

Daughter: [Deep breath for this very long run-on sentence said with conviction] … I don't know what my new *church situation* is going to be after we move, and I do know I'm not going to have the same friends and relationships that I have with my small group and my small group leader now, and missing one for me means a ton because we have no idea how long it will be until we move and I have no idea how many more small groups I'll be *blessed* to have.

Dad: [No further response]

You've got to hand it to this young lady. It was a full-court press. But the dad remained firm and loving in his decision. Many parents wring their hands in worry as they contemplate how to parent their children and the decisions they are making. We want spiritually healthy families, but sometimes making it a practical pursuit each day can get muddled if we don't pause to commemorate, "this far we have made it."

My husband and I were two of these parents. We desired to be godly parents, and we knew we would need insight from God and His Word on how to raise our children in a way that would help them successfully enter their adult years—not just physically and socially, but also spiritually. We wanted milestones to check our progress.

Our Spiritual Roots

The Jewish Bar and Bat Mitzvah celebrations have their roots in the Old Testament and have since become cultural rites of passage for those in the Jewish faith. It's also important to note that these elaborate parties also have significant spiritual roots. They date back to a time when the Jewish people were scattered all over the world due to persecution. Jewish leaders wanted to teach their children the Hebrew language so they could study the Torah (the first five books of the Bible that constitute the Law). Not wanting to see their faith extinguished, the leaders made the synagogue schools into the primary means for the instruction of reading, writing, and speaking the Hebrew language.

My husband, Dr. Michael Anthony, explained it this way:

> Young boys attended [synagogue] once they reached the age of manhood at thirteen.[1]

> This rite of passage entitled the boy to privileges and responsibilities of adult men, such as serving with other men in the synagogue and in the courts.... Only boys were allowed to participate in formal education [at this time], and older boys from the tribe of Levi were apprenticed by older priests.[2]

The Jewish community understood the value of "endorsing" the young men in their community as they entered adulthood through teaching, opportunities, mentoring, and the entrustment of responsibility. We have much to learn from their practices.

A Modern Perspective

Jeremy Lee, the creator of parentministry.net and former youth pastor of more than twenty years, recounted watching a modern manhood ceremony that he was invited to attend:

> A dad invited about five or six guys who had been influential in his son's life to celebrate the son's 18th birthday. During the ceremony, we all took turns sharing words of encouragement with the young man. And then it was the dad's turn.
>
> He asked his son to kneel down. Then he went to the closet and brought out a huge *Braveheart*-looking sword. When I saw the sword, I was genuinely afraid. I had no idea what was happening. I was afraid I was about to witness some weird circumcision ceremony or something.
>
> Then the dad laid the sword on his son's shoulder. And I will never forget what he said next.
>
> "I have friends who are 30 and 40 years old who act like boys, because no one ever told them that they were a man. Son, based on the authority given to me by God's Word, as your dad, I tell you that you knelt down as a boy, but you rise as a man."

I wish you could have seen the look on that son's face. I wish you could have seen the look on that *father's* face. The transfer of Blessing that took place in that moment was the most powerful parental exchange I had ever witnessed. That young man would never wonder if he had his dad's approval. His dad unleashed him into the world with confidence, support, and biblical foundation.[3]

What a powerful moment for that family. The cost required the purchase of a sword. The preparation required the writing of some words of affirmation and the inviting of some friends. But the *value* of this moment for that son was *priceless*.

Passing Down Faith

Jeremy Lee recognizes that the idea of parents passing down their faith to their children can be intimidating. He says it's often a recipe for a freak-out moment when parents realize that their child's view of God largely comes from what he or she learns at home. When faced with an intimidating task like that, Jeremy notes that we typically have one of these responses:

- We become paralyzed, ignore it, and do nothing.
- We overcompensate and do more than we need to do.
- We hand our kid a book and hope they figure it out.

- We delegate the task to someone else and hope it
works out for the best.

Yet we don't have to fall into those failing responses. Instead, we can look to Scripture and the character of God for insights on living. In a conversation with Lee, he shared, "After many of the great movements of God, He asked His people to build a memorial so that they would remember what He had done. God created a system of spiritual ceremonies for His people to celebrate regularly as families to remember what He had done. When Jesus was on His way to the cross, He used the symbols of wine and bread to teach about what was going to happen to Him. Then He invited His followers to 'do this in remembrance of [Him]' as a ceremony to help them remember."

Ours is a God who has placed symbols, rituals, and community celebrations in our lives intentionally to help us remember. One of the most prominent examples of this in Scripture is the celebration of annual feasts (or festivals). We see that children in the Bible participated in the festivals every year, where they enjoyed the faith community in all its richness. They ate delicious food, learned and joined in cultural dances, and shared a common experience with people they hadn't seen in months perhaps—cousins, friends, and family members from all over the region. They'd come together to celebrate for somewhere between seven and ten days!

Those days together in the faith community were rich marker points of faith development, as it would have been a spiritually shaping experience for kids to have lived in that type of communal expression of worship. So how do we create these markers of both physical and spiritual growth that our children need? How do we ensure that we're being diligent in creating this type of environment and community for their development? Let's take a look at how we might translate the goodness of God's character and His plan into traditions for the modern family.

And, by the way, this idea of remembering and celebrating certain rites of passage is not merely limited to the rearing of our children either. Of course we want to create intentional markers for them, but many times this practice must start with the parents, living out and modeling the life that God has in mind for us.

Traditions: Remember and Celebrate

In my book *Dreaming of More for the Next Generation*, I share a story of how my husband and I were awakened to the beauty of creating a "passage":

> Recently my husband and I celebrated our wedding anniversary. Usually we go out to dinner and exchange gifts or cards. However, this time we decided to introduce this concept of Remember and Celebrate into our evening. At dinner, I took out a napkin and wrote down the ways God had showed His faithfulness to us in each year of our lives together. After we completed the list of remembrance, the only response was celebration and worship! It was the most meaningful anniversary

we have ever experienced simply because we took
the time to stop, to pause … and remember.[4]

God ordained this kind of rhythm because active remembrance
cultivates *relationship*. God wants us to look back and recognize His
faithfulness, intense love, and personal interaction with His people
individually and as a community. When we teach children to pause
and remember, we teach them what it means to honor their relationships with God—those intimate relationships in which our children
speak and He listens; He speaks and our children respond.

One family I know engages in this type of tradition on an almost
nightly basis. It's a milestone of God's provision for just that one day!
Think about it. Each day we have the opportunity as we watch the
sun set to give thanks for life and breath. To glorify God for who He
is. As this family sits around the dinner table, each person reflects on
his or her day.

As each person recounts the ways he saw Jesus in his life that day,
he pauses to remember. Then in an act of celebration, the whole family raises their glasses (of milk, juice, or water) and cheers, "To Jesus!"
This fun and impromptu tradition allows young family members to
see God's power working in everyday and ordinary life situations as
well as life's bigger spiritual milestones.

Spiritual Scrapbooks

When my kids were young, I enjoyed scrapbooking. In many ways,
creating pages full of photos, stickers, and colorful paper highlight-
ing my family's events was a way to remember and celebrate the

milestones of the past year. In recent years our "scrapbooks" look like a video year-in-review slide show. Either way, my adult children still love pulling out those old scrapbooks and DVDs to recount the goodness of those moments in their lives.

In chapter 7 of *A Theology for Family Ministry*, Dr. Leon Blanchette makes several great observations. Below is a summary of his thoughts:

> Spiritual milestones serve the Christian in much the same way a scrapbook serves as a reminder of important moments in one's life. Pictures and mementos of significant moments of life are recorded for future remembrance. A lock of hair from a child's first haircut, a picture with a group of friends on a retreat, the love note from a dear friend, and the Bible given by your grandparents all serve as reminders of moments that are never to be forgotten.... These mementos remind one who they are and where they are from. They serve as reminders of God's faithfulness through tough times and good.
>
> The same is true for spiritual milestones. There are key moments in the spiritual life of a child. These moments have the potential to change the trajectory of a child's journey for a lifetime. Significant moments not only serve as milestones on the journey with God but also serve as a way for parents and the church to gauge the spiritual development of their children. As children participate in key biblical

milestones, they create mementos that are placed in the spiritual scrapbook of their lives. These moments in time are captured in these scrapbooks as reminders of their journey with God and serve as an encouragement to continue the faithful journey with Christ. In those moments of discouragement, despair, and doubt, this scrapbook of biblical milestones will be the encouragement that challenges them to continue on the journey with Christ.[5]

Blanchette encourages that "this scrapbook of a Christian child's life should include snapshots of the following biblical milestones, moments that are significant in the spiritual development of a child": [6]

Confession of Faith: Conversion
"If you declare with your mouth, 'Jesus is Lord', and believe in your heart that God raised him from the dead, you will be saved." (Rom. 10:9)

Baptism
"Therefore go and make disciples of all nations, baptizing them in the name of the Father and of the Son and of the Holy Spirit." (Matt. 28:19)

Communion: The Lord's Supper
"And he took bread, gave thanks and broke it, and gave it to them, saying, 'This is my body given for you; do this in remembrance of me'." (Luke 22:19)

The Great Commission: Evangelism

"Therefore go and make disciples of all nations." (Matt. 28:19)

Service

"Each of you should use whatever gift you have received to serve others, as faithful stewards of God's grace in its various forms." (1 Pet. 4:10)[7]

Often, churches set up programs and classes to allow children and even their parents to participate in these milestones. My encouragement is to take what is offered and then make it your own. If your church offers baptism classes and a baptism ceremony, allow the church to equip and support you in this spiritual milestone, but also think of creative ways to make these moments special to your family.

Personalizing Milestones

In *Spiritual Parenting*, I share the story of my own son's baptism:

> When my kids made the decision to be baptized, we wanted to share this experience with others who had been participants and eyewitnesses to their lives. For each of their celebrations, we let them be the ones who assembled the guest list. At my son's baptism celebration, we had many friends and neighbors who did not know Jesus personally or belong to a faith community.

> We gathered at the beach for my son to
> be baptized in the ocean. After the baptism
> we gathered to bless him by speaking words of
> encouragement to him. Some shared how they
> had seen God working in his life or had observed
> special gifts that God had given to him in order to
> bless others. Some read verses of encouragement,
> and others prayed for him. It was a meaningful
> day for my son to hear so many strengthening
> words by those who knew and loved him. When
> it was finished, his grandfather closed in a prayer
> of blessing.[8]

That is a day my son has never forgotten. It was a day that ushered him, in an official and personal way, deeper into his faith journey.

I share this story because, while the church provided the training and the organization of the baptism itself, my husband and I made it *personal for our son*. We lived near the beach, and he loves the ocean, so we did it there. We allowed him to select the people who would be there—much to our surprise we found people on his list that we hadn't thought to invite. And they came!

We asked individuals to write words of blessing ahead of time to either read aloud or write in a card as a keepsake. We coordinated a potluck-style meal and shared dinner together—complete with s'mores. And then we asked the patriarch of our family to close our time in prayer and blessing. Each of these things made this spiritual milestone personal for our son and added a page to his spiritual scrapbook.

Milestones of Life

There are other types of milestones that can be celebrated in addition to the biblical ones. Some families determine a certain age when the children in their family receive their first Bible. During those early elementary years when a child is reading on her own, the gift of God's Word can be a sacred marker of faith. Parents can host a special dinner and share their own favorite verses and encourage their child with ways that God's Word has impacted their own lives.

Other ideas include taking a mission trip to a different country or participating in a local mission for a day or longer, setting up an account for putting aside tithes and offerings after a young adult gets his first job, and receiving a purity ring in adolescence when a teenager determines to keep herself pure until marriage.

My daughter was fourteen when we decided that her declaration of purity would be a meaningful rite of passage. My husband and I found a beautiful ring that held her birthstone. This ring was a token of her identity and purity before God. My husband and I chose a time and asked her to be a part of a special ceremony that we had planned for her.

When we gathered together, my husband gave our daughter her ring. He spoke words of blessing to her and validated her worth and beauty in his—and more importantly, in God's—eyes. He affirmed her desire to stay pure until she was married but also cautioned her that it would be difficult and that she would need to stay close to Jesus as the source of her strength to accomplish this.

I handed her a Styrofoam cup and asked her to hold it. I told her that many guys would want to be with her, and that those boys would be as common as the cup she was holding. They could be found anywhere. There are millions of them—everywhere. I also reminded her that a Styrofoam cup is for a single use and is easily *tossed away after it is used.*

Next, I handed her a golden teacup. It was radiant. In fact, it was hand painted and therefore one-of-a-kind. This cup, I told her, is something that you keep and treasure. You are careful and honoring of it because you *value* it. This would represent the kind of man in marriage that we wanted her to wait for when giving herself sexually. We hugged her, told her that we loved her unconditionally, and then prayed with her. That ring remained on her finger and that teacup in clear view throughout the rest of the years that she lived in our home to serve as symbolic reminders of the ceremony of blessing and passage that we had shared together.

Getting Started

The reality is that our children will grow up and be gone before we know it. The brevity of time we have to influence their confidence, security, and most importantly their faith demands that we *must have a plan* to make sure their path will be secured with memorable markers and events.

Take some time to answer the questions in the "reflect and respond" section at the end of this chapter. Then prayerfully ask God to grant you the wisdom and strength to put these plans into action. I encourage you to not get distracted by making this more than it needs to be or by *minimizing* the lifelong—even eternal—impact it will assuredly have on your child's life.

Jon Nielson, a college pastor in Illinois, has made it his life's endeavor to encourage parents and the church to work together and not give up in the spiritual formation of this generation. He does remind us that we can never make our efforts formulaic, however. He wrote:

> Kids from wonderful gospel-centered homes leave the church; people from messed-up family backgrounds find eternal life in Jesus and have beautiful marriages and families. But it's also not a crap-shoot. In general, children who are led in their faith during their growing-up years by parents who love Jesus vibrantly, serve their church actively, and saturate their home with the gospel completely, grow up to love Jesus and the church. The words of Proverbs 22:6 do not constitute a formula that is true 100 percent of the time, but they do provide us with a principle that comes from the gracious plan of God, the God who delights to see his gracious Word passed from generation to generation: "Train up a child in the way he should go; even when he is old he will not depart from it."[9]

We desire to have spiritually healthy families and to be the kind of parents that God intended when He entrusted our children to us. As you embark on the next leg of your journey, whether you are just beginning your family or you are almost finished with child-rearing, let me encourage you with this final blessing:

Families, may you be filled with the love and knowledge of our Lord Jesus Christ, who is at work in and through you. May you understand afresh the role He has graciously entrusted to you in the children who are in your home. As you seek to build a spiritually healthy family, may you be encouraged and strengthened by the power of God's Spirit to not grow weary and to not give up. Be strong and courageous and give thanks to God in all things. And now to Him who is able to accomplish more than we can think or imagine, to Him be the glory forever and ever. Amen.

Reflect and Respond

1. In what ways were rites of passage displayed in your life growing up? Which, if any, have marked the person you are today? What was it about that passage or event that had such an impact on you?

2. As you look at the five biblical rites of passage—Conversion, Baptism, Communion, Evangelism, and Service—which passages are you still looking forward to celebrating with each of your children? In what ways can you enhance these experiences to make them memorable, spiritually healthy markers?

3. What other life passages will occur in your family? First day of school, receiving a first Bible, getting a driver's license, ushering into adulthood? Which ones are particularly special to your family that you want to celebrate? How can you begin to imagine and plan how those days or events might look?

4. Why is it important to you to make these spiritual markers a priority in your family amid all that is clamoring for your attention? What are you willing to sacrifice in order to make these dreams realities for your child?

APPENDIX A

The Ten Environments

---

1. Storytelling

The Big God Story gives us an accurate and awe-inspiring perspective into how God has been moving throughout history. It is the story of redemption, salvation, and hope, and tells how we have been grafted into it by grace. It further compels us to see how God is using every person's life and is creating a unique story that deserves to be told for His glory.

"God has a big story, and I can be a part of it!"

2. Identity

This environment highlights who we are in Christ. According to Ephesians 1, we have been chosen, adopted, redeemed, sealed, and given inheritances in Christ—all of which we did nothing to earn. This conviction allows children to stand firm against the destructive counter identities the world offers.

"I belong to God, and He loves me!"

3. Faith Community

God designed us to live in community and to experience Him in ways that can happen only in proximity to one another. The faith community creates an environment to equip and disciple parents, to celebrate God's faithfulness, and to bring a richness of worship through tradition and rituals that offer children an identity. Our love for each other reflects the love we have received from God.

"God's family cares for one another and worships God together."

4. Service

This posture of the heart asks the question, "What needs to be done?" It allows the Holy Spirit to cultivate in us a sensitivity to others and helps us focus on a cause bigger than our individual lives. Serving others helps us fulfill the mandate as Christ-followers to view our lives as living sacrifices that we generously give away.

"What needs to be done?"

5. Out of the Comfort Zone

As children and students are challenged to step out of their comfort zones from an early age, they experience a dependence on the Holy Spirit to equip and strengthen them beyond their natural abilities and desires. We believe this environment will cultivate a generation of individuals who, instead of seeking comfort, seek radical lives of faith in Christ.

"God transforms me when I step out in faith."

6. Responsibility

This environment captures the ability to take ownership of our lives, gifts, and resources before God. A child must be challenged to take responsibility for his or her brothers and sisters in Christ, as well as for those who are spiritually lost. We hope the Holy Spirit will use this environment to allow us to understand that God has entrusted His world to each of His children.

"God has entrusted me with the things and people He created around me."

7. Course Correction

This environment flows out of Hebrews 12:11–13 and is the direct opposite of punishment. Instead, biblical discipline for a child encompasses a season of pain, then building up in love, followed by a vision of a corrected path—all with the purpose of healing at its core.

"When I get off track, God offers me a path of healing."

8. Love and Respect

Without love, our faith is futile. Children need an environment of love and respect in order to be free to both receive and give God's grace. This environment declares that children are respected because they embody the image of God. We must speak *to* our children, not *at* them, and we must commit to an environment where love and acceptance are never withheld due to a child's behavior.

"God fills me with His love so I can give it away."

9. Knowing

Nothing could be more important than knowing and being known by God. We live in a world that denies absolute truth, yet God's Word offers just that. As we create an environment that upholds and displays God's truth, we give children a foundation based on knowing God, His Word, and a relationship with Him through Christ. God is holy, mighty, and awesome, yet He has chosen to make Himself known to us!

"God knows me, and I can know Him."

10. Modeling

Biblical content requires a practical, living expression in order for it to be spiritually influential. This environment gives hands-on examples of what it means for children to put their faith into action. Modeling puts flesh on faith and reminds us that others are watching to see if we live what we believe.

"I see Christ in others, and they can see Him in me."

APPENDIX B

*Questions to Consider in Writing
a Family Mission Statement*

- What kind of family life do you want your children to remember?
- What kind of atmosphere do you want to have in your home?
- What kind of family do you want to be known for?
- What kind of parent do you want to be?
- What behaviors do you want your family members to demonstrate?
- What goals will you have for your children at various stages of their lives?
- What are some of your fondest childhood memories?
- What painful experiences did you have in your family that you do not feel would benefit your children if replicated?
- What kinds of biblical qualities do you believe children should exhibit?
- What mode of discipline do you feel is best in your home?
- What changes do you need to make in order to allow your family to have more time/fun together?

- What perspectives should your children encounter other than the ones that they are naturally exposed to? (Think of culture, economics, politics, and so on.)
- What are you willing to sacrifice in order to accomplish these plans?

APPENDIX C

Writing a Mission Statement

But those who plan what is good find love and faithfulness.
Proverbs 14:22

1. As you begin to think through your mission statement, write down three things that you want for your family and children as an *end result*. What do you hope to see when they are young adults someday? (For example, to live lives in accordance with God's laws and grace, to reflect the character of God, to demonstrate a life of love, and so on.) These are essentially value statements.

   Write them here:

   _____

   _____

   _____

   _____

   _____

   _____

2. Think about these desires and visions for your family that you just wrote down. In what ways could you be a part of that end result? Think of three words that give you a place in that. Words such as: *model, nurture, encourage and hold accountable, demonstrate, come alongside of, inspire,* and so on.

Attach these words to the prior vision words (in question 1) and then begin to add *linking words* (such as *through, and, with, for*). Write a rough draft and don't overthink it—you can always revise later.

Pray about your participation in your child's spiritual growth and write your thoughts on question 2 here:

_____

_____

_____

_____

_____

_____

3. Using your answers from questions 1 and 2, begin to write your family mission statement here:

_____

_____

_____

_____

_____

_____

Example:

We, the _____ family, will endeavor, with God's help, to model lives that are lived in accordance with God's laws and grace, to come alongside those who are poor, both in life and spirit, and to nurture our children to reflect the character of God by demonstrating a life of love in all circumstances.

Notes

Chapter 3—Kissing the World Good-Bye

1. C. S. Lewis, *The Screwtape Letters*, (New York, NY: Harper Collins, 1942), 44.

Chapter 4—Free Indeed

1. Adapted from Don Carter, "Enabling Behavior—Loving Too Much," *Internet of the Mind*, www.internet-of-the-mind.com/enabling_behavior.html.

2. Carter, "Enabling Behavior."

3. Jim Burns, *Creating an Intimate Marriage: Rekindle Romance Through Affection, Warmth and Encouragement* (Grand Rapids, MI: Bethany, 2007), 159.

4. Gary Thomas, *The Sacred Search: What If It's Not about Who You Marry, But Why?* (Colorado Springs, CO: David C Cook, 2013), 18.

Chapter 5—Beyond the Pursuit of Perfection

1. Randy Frazee, *The Heart of the Story* (Grand Rapids, MI: Zondervan, 2011), 18–19.

2. Dictionary.com, s.v. "Usurp," dictionary.reference.com.

Chapter 7—A Time to Bless

1. Jill Carattini, "On Blessing," RZIM.org, October 10, 2014, www.rzim.org/a-slice-of-infinity/on-blessing/, emphasis added.

2. Carattini, "On Blessing."

3. Gary Smalley and John Trent, *The Blessing: Giving the Gift of Unconditional Love and Acceptance* (Nashville, TN: Thomas Nelson).

Chapter 8—Living a Meaningful Family Mission

1. "In-N-Out Burger," 123HelpMe.com, www.123HelpMe.com/view.asp?id =165565.

Chapter 9—Beyond Good Behavior and Chore Charts

1. Barrett Johnson, "How to Raise a Pagan Kid in a Christian Home," *Info for Families*, November 13, 2013, www.infoforfamilies.com /blog/2013/11/13/how-to-raise-a-pagan-kid-in-a-christian-home#.U_ EbXuBETwc=.

2. Dr. John H. Coe, "Resisting the Temptation of Moral Formation: Moving from Moral to Spiritual Formation" (Talbot Theological Seminary, 2007), www.biola.edu/spiritualformation/media/downloads/lecture/Temptation %20Outline.pdf. Used with permission.

3. Ruth Haley Barton, *Strengthening the Soul of Your Leadership: Seeking God in the Crucible of Ministry* (Downers Grove, IL: InterVarsity Press, 2008), 16.

4. M. Robert Mulholland Jr., *Invitation to a Journey: A Road Map for Spiritual Formation* (Downers Grove, IL: InterVarsity Press, 1993), 12.

Chapter 10—Remember and Celebrate the Abundant Life

1. Michael J. Anthony, *Exploring the History and Philosophy of Christian Education: Principles for the 21st Century* (Grand Rapids, MI: Kregel, 2003), 35.

2. Michael J. Anthony and Michelle Anthony, *A Theology for Family Ministries* (Nashville, TN: B&H, 2011), 226.

3 Jeremy Lee, "The Story Behind Parent Ministry.net," ParentMinistry. net, September 20, 2103, parentministry.net/2013/09/the-story-behind -parentministry-net/.

4. Michelle Anthony, *Dreaming of More for the Next Generation: Lifetime Faith Ignited by Family Ministry* (Colorado Springs, CO: David C Cook, 2012), 145–46.

5. Leon Blanchette in Michael J. and Michelle Anthony, *A Theology of Family Ministry* (Nashville, TN: Broadman and Holman, 2011), 119.

6. Blanchette, *Theology of Family Ministry*, 125.

7. Adapted from Blanchette, *Theology of Family Ministry*, 125, 129, 131, 132, 133.

8. Michelle Anthony, *Spiritual Parenting: An Awakening for Today's Families* (Colorado Springs, CO: David C Cook, 2010), 96.

9. Jon Nielson, "Why Youth Stay in Church When They Grow Up," *The Gospel Coalition*, July 29, 2011, www.thegospelcoalition.org/article/why -youth-stay-in-church-when-they-grow-up/.

INVITE YOUR KIDS INTO GOD'S BIG STORY

THE BIG GOD STORY

MICHELLE ANTHONY

Illustrated by Cory Godbey

In this fast-paced journey through God's Big Story, kids will hear about the Redeemer and follow His story from the garden of Eden through the promise of His return. Ultimately, readers will see where they fit into God's Big Story of love when they write their names on the last page of the book!

BE EMPOWERD IN YOUR ROLE AS A PARENT!

Spiritual Parenting is a six-part program that empowers parents to be the primary nurturers of their children's faith. Families will be transformed as they learn how to create space for God-encounters in everyday life.

Perfect for parenting classes, mom groups, mid-week, retreats, and more!

Envision
a NEW GENERATION
who know GOD'S WORD, desire to OBEY HIM, and respond to god through the POWER of the HOLY SPIRIT

You are impassioned for a new generation and believe that God wants to captivate the hearts of today's children and families. *Tru Curriculum offers the ministry resources that will allow you to have confidence that you are developing lifetime faith in a new generation.*

 trū | David C Cook
transforming lives together